WIRRAL PUBS

LES JONES

AMBERLEY

In memory of Paul 'Deaks' Deakin
A true friend, greatly missed

First published 2025

Amberley Publishing
The Hill, Stroud
Gloucestershire, GL5 4EP

www.amberley-books.com

ISBN 978 1 3981 1421 0 (print)
ISBN 978 1 3981 1422 7 (ebook)

British Library Cataloguing in Publication Data.
A catalogue record for this book is available from the British Library.

Typesetting by SJmagic DESIGN SERVICES, India.
Printed in the UK.

EU GPSR Authorised Representative
Appointed EU Representative: Easy Access System Europe Oü, 16879218
Address: Mustamäe tee 50, 10621, Tallinn, Estonia
Contact Details: gpsr.requests@easproject.com, +358 40 500 3575

Contents

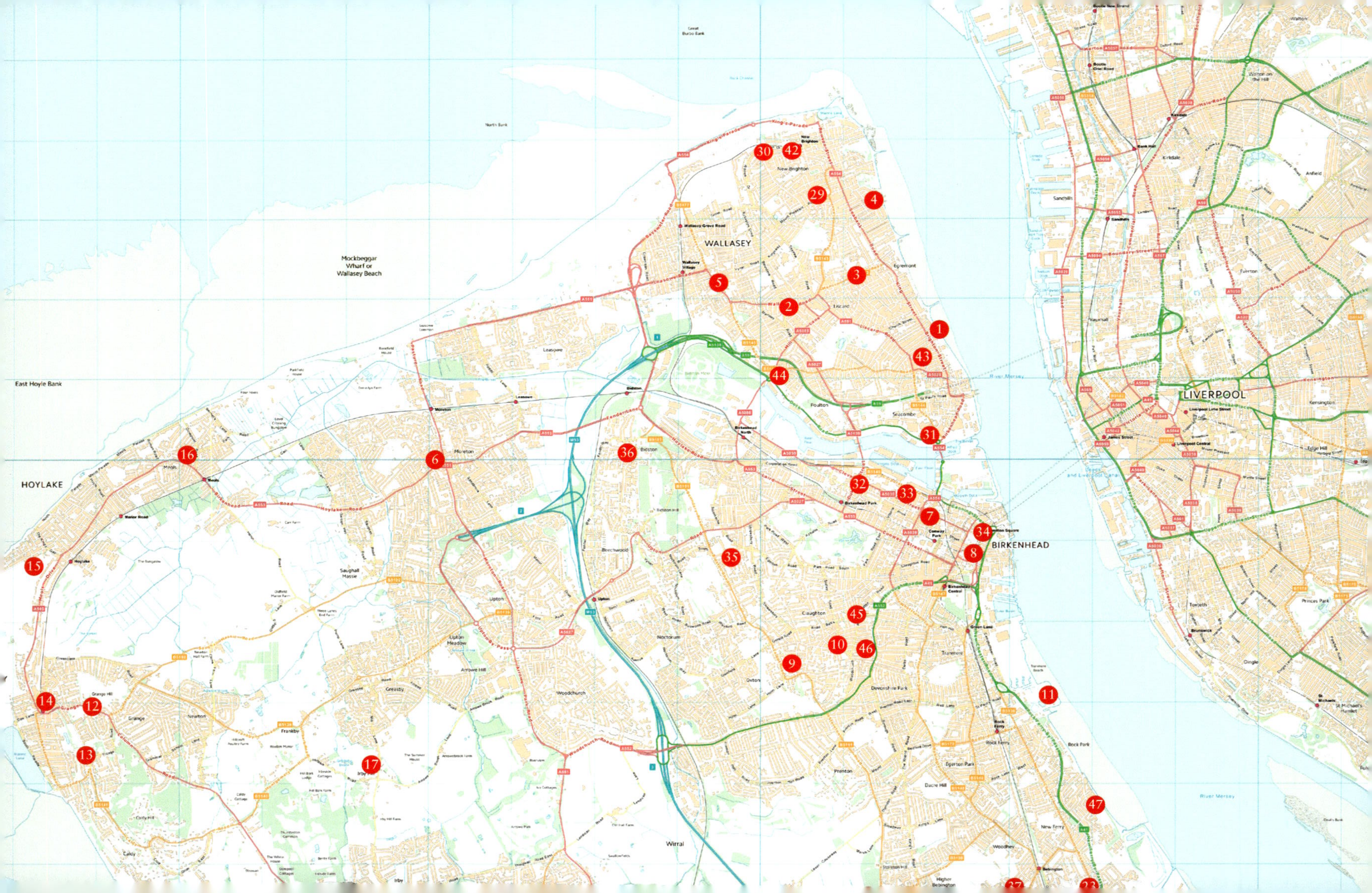
LIVERPOOL
BIRKENHEAD
WALLASEY
HOYLAKE
Mockbeggar
Wharf or
Wallasey Beach
East Hoyle Bank
River Mersey
New Brighton
Egremont
Liscard
Seacombe
Poulton
Leasowe
Moreton
Bidston
Upton
Claughton
Oxton
Noctorum
Woodchurch
Greasby
Frankby
Irby
Newton
Grange
Caldy
Tranmere
Rock Ferry
Devonshire Park
Prenton
Dacre Hill
Egerton Park
Wirral
Toxteth
Dingle
Kirkdale
Everton
Anfield
Kensington
Sandhills
Saughall
Massie
Upton
Meadow
Arrowe Hill
Birchwood
New Ferry
Bebington
1
2
3
4
5
6
7
8
9
10
11
12
13
14
15
16
17
29
30
31
32
33
34
35
36
42
43
44
45
46
47

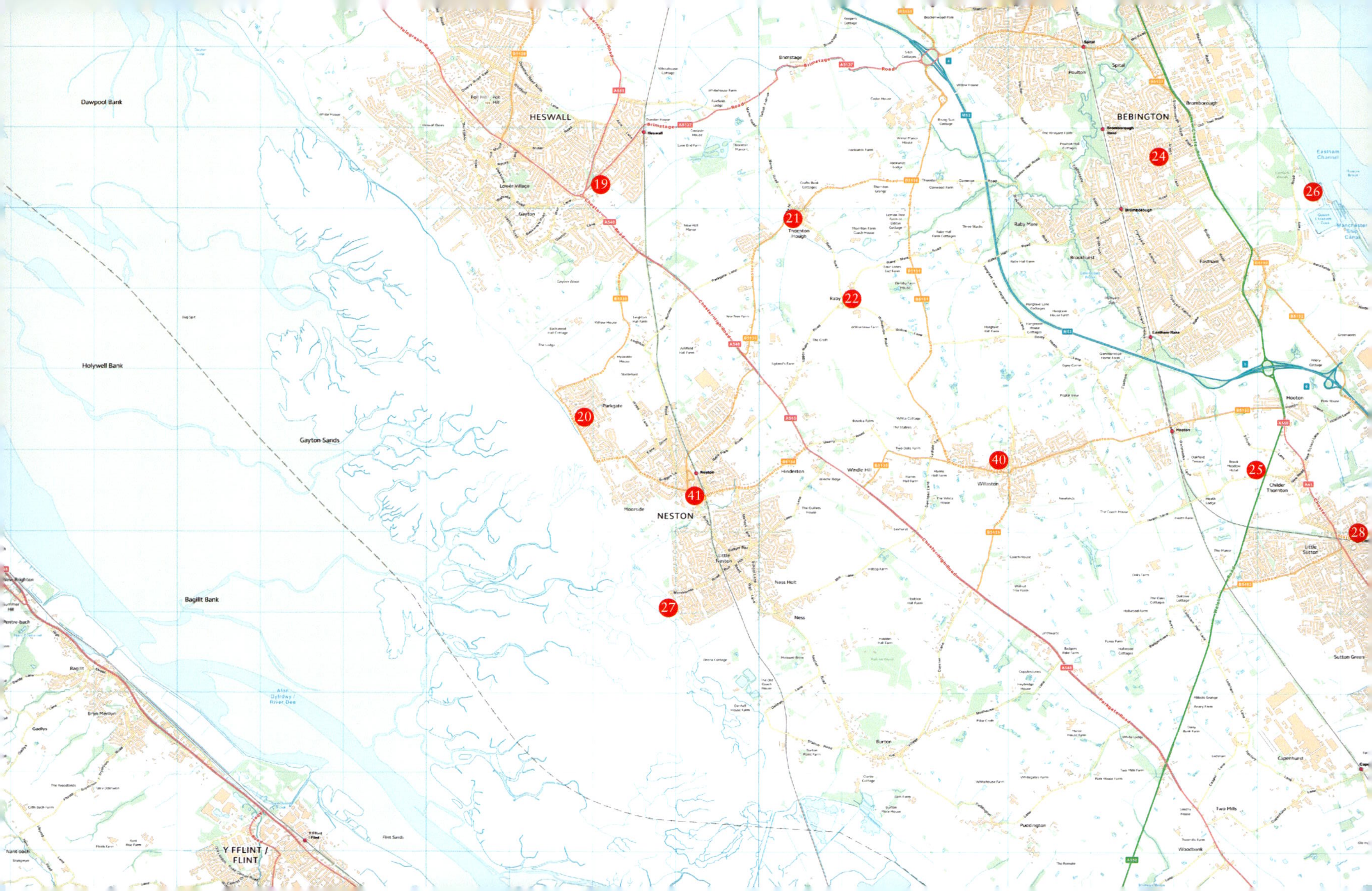

HESWALL
NESTON
BEBINGTON
Y FFLINT / FLINT
Dawpool Bank
Holywell Bank
Gayton Sands
Bagillt Bank
Parkgate
Thornton Hough
Raby
Willaston
Hooton
Childer Thornton
Little Sutton
Little Neston
Ness Holt
Ness
Burton
Puddington
Capenhurst
Two Mills
Woodbank
Sutton Green
Brimstage
Poulton
Spital
Bromborough
Eastham
Raby Mere
Brackhurst
Lower Village
Gayton
Moorside
Hinderton
Windle Hill
Bagillt
Gadlys
Eastham Channel
Chester High Road
Parkgate Road
Brimstage Road
Telegraph Road
Chester Road
19
20
21
22
24
25
26
27
28
40
41

Key

1. The Egremont Ferry, Egremont
2. The Boot Inn, Liscard
3. The Primrose, Liscard
4. The Magazine Hotel, New Brighton
5. The Cheshire Cheese, Wallasey Village
6. The Coach and Horses, Moreton
7. The Stork, Birkenhead
8. Gallaghers, Birkenhead
9. The Queens Arms, Oxton
10. The Shrewsbury Arms, Oxton
11. The Refreshment Rooms, Rock Ferry
12. The White Lion, West Kirby
13. The Ring O' Bells, West Kirby
14. The Dee Hotel, West Kirby
15. The Green Lodge, Hoylake
16. The Railway Inn, Meols
17. The Irby Mill, Greasby
18. The Fox and Hounds, Barnston
19. The Glegg Arms, Gayton
20. The Red Lion, Parkgate
21. The Seven Stars, Thornton Hough
22. The Wheatsheaf, Raby
23. The Bridge Inn, Port Sunlight
24. The Bromborough Hotel, Bromborough
25. The White Lion, Childer Thornton
26. The Eastham Ferry
27. The Harp, Little Neston
28. The Olde Red Lion, Little Sutton
29. The Little Brighton, New Brighton
30. The Albion Hotel, New Brighton
31. The Swan, Seacombe
32. The Grand Trunk, Birkenhead
33. The Meadows, Birkenhead
34. The Pier Hotel, Birkenhead
35. The Chetwynd Arms, Oxton
36. The Ring O' Bells, Bidston
37. The Dog and Gun, Bebington
38. The Gladstone Arms, Bebington
39. The Royal Oak, Bebington
40. The Red Lion, Willaston
41. The Coach and Horses, Neston
42. The Hotel Victoria, New Brighton
43. The Dale, Seacombe
44. The Jolly Sailor, Poulton
45. The Grange, Birkenhead
46. The Happy Valley, Birkenhead
47. The Great Eastern, New Ferry

Introduction

'If more of us valued food and cheer above hoarded gold, it would be a merrier world.'
J. R. R. Tolkien

The English public house is one of the great British institutions, envied throughout the world. There are many fine watering holes in countries near and far, but nothing compares with the good old English pub with its mixture of hospitality, conviviality and history moulded seamlessly into a unique whole.

Pubs nationally, however, have been closing at a rate of four per week over the last ten years and this relentless attrition is unfortunately reflected in Wirral, which now has 700 fewer pubs than during its heyday at the turn of the last century. Furthermore, according to figures released by CAMRA, less than 4 per cent of pubs in England retain interiors of any real historical value, with genuine fabric being torn out and picturesque nooks and crannies removed, to be replaced by faux beams and plastic seating. Even the name of the pub has often been changed such as 'The Red Lion' becoming 'The Frog and Radiator' for no other reason than the whim of a humourless marketing executive with red braces and no friends.

This sorry state of affairs has thankfully slowed recently and an appreciation for what remains is being driven by an upsurge in popularity for cask and craft ales and the growth in microbreweries. Local brewers of real ales such as Peerless and Brimstage have been recently joined by craft ale brewers Glen Affric, which all augers well for the future.

The pub is one of the most recognisable symbols of Englishness we possess, but it is of surprisingly recent origin, being a predominantly Victorian invention. We have to go back to pre-Conquest times to find the earliest examples of what would evolve into the public house we know and love. The original ale houses sold ale (a mixture of malt and water) to the local populace. The inn appeared around the fourteenth century to cater for travellers and pilgrims, and provided a bed for the night and stabling if required. These country pubs were perfectly suited for the English and their pace of life for many centuries, but this pedestrian idyll was about to change forever.

The shock of the Industrial Revolution caused an exodus of people from the country into the booming towns and cities and these hordes of thirsty workers required servicing. This was the Victorians time to shine and as with much of what the Victorians did, they took to the task with gusto. Public houses appeared on practically every street corner in the burgeoning industrial towns, with Birkenhead being a prime example – fifteen were built along Cleveland Street alone. Most were modest affairs with a public bar and a slightly more comfortable parlour but little else. Others provided accommodation above the premises for travelling salesmen, usually consisting of two or three beds but being grandly titled hotel. Larger pubs followed, originally catering for large groups of workers centred around the likes of Cammell Lairds where men would stream out of the yard and straight into the Castle Hotel opposite where serried rows of beer had already been pulled, ready for the inevitable invasion of thirsty fitters, all gagging for a bevvy.

The largest pubs on Wirral, however, were built in the twentieth century when car ownership began to increase and the huge road pubs such as the Arrowe Park Hotel, the Railway Hotel at Meols and the Coach and Horses in Moreton, which were constructed to service the passing motorist.

Wirral has examples of pubs in all these myriad guises, and they should all be treasured and, more to the point, patronised, even if it means putting down this book and paying your local a visit. They are ideal places to meet friends and socialise with your drink of choice, to enjoy a snack or a meal out, to combat loneliness or to chill out generally.

I hope you enjoy my selection and apologise if your favourite tavern has not been included.

Wirral Pubs

1. The Egremont Ferry, Egremont

The arrival of the ferry boats from Liverpool had a profound effect on the Wirral side of the Mersey. Landing stages were erected at Seacombe, Egremont and New Brighton in the Wallasey district, along with many more upstream. The ferry at Egremont was championed by slaver and sometime ferryman Captain John Askew and built to his specifications in 1827, the surrounding area becoming known from his birthplace in what was then Cumberland and is now part of Cumbria.

Originally named The Egremont Tap as there was a public house called The Ferry Hotel in nearby Tobin Street, the pub was originally a Free House until Bents bought the property in 1900, followed by local brewers Higsons. It was able to change its name to the Egremont Ferry in 1925 when the premises in Tobin Street closed down.

Being sited roughly halfway between Seacombe and New Brighton, the 'Eggy', as it was known locally, was ideally placed to garner passing trade from the thousands of day trippers who took the ferry from Liverpool to Seacombe en route to New Brighton, saving themselves a couple of pennies by not taking a ferry directly to New Brighton. It is a couple of miles between Seacombe and New Brighton and all this walking would make one thirsty of course, so many would then stop off for a quick pint at the Eggy, possibly following time-honoured tradition of leaving the tribe of kids outside with a bottle of pop – but no crisps as they had yet to be invented. The diversion into the pub would often be made on the return trip as well; while dad was inside the rest of the family may have popped down onto the sands as this particular stretch of sand was rarely covered by the Mersey.

The view from the pub took in the ferry itself, before this was removed after being hit for the umpteenth time by a coaster one foggy day in 1946. Granted it was the longest pier on the Mersey but ships captains should really have been paying more attention. The ferry buildings struggled on for many years after, the right side of the complex being allocated as the local speakers corner and some of the old ferry buildings being used as a nightclub called Davey Jones Locker. When they were finally pulled down seats were provided for patrons of the Eggy to drink alfresco.

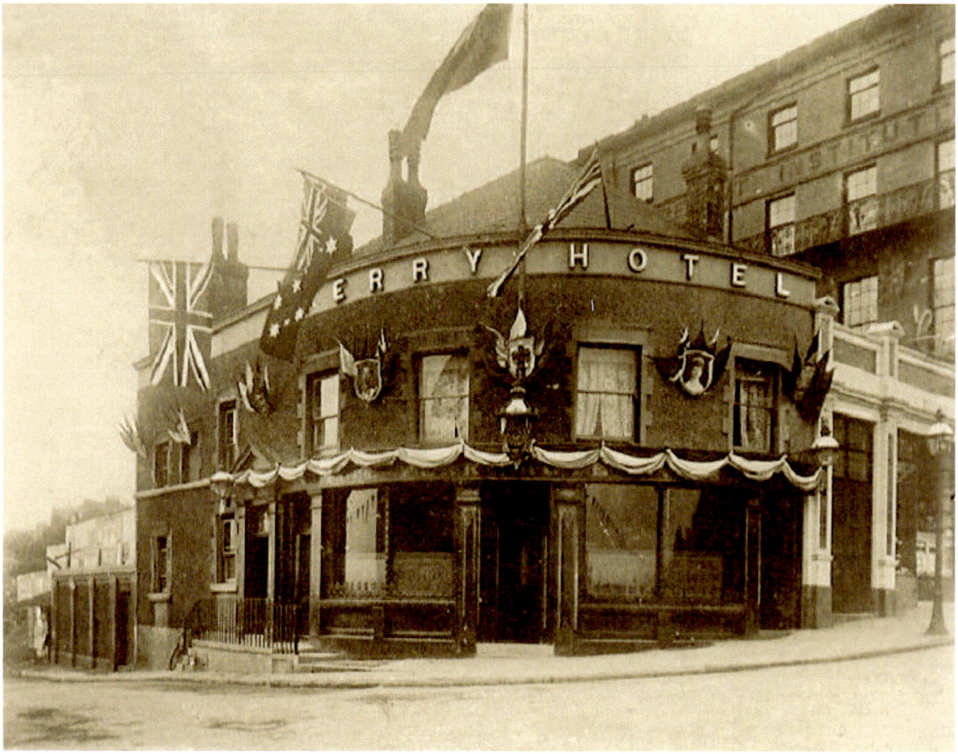

Celebrations at The Egremont Ferry for the Coronation of Edward VII in 1911.

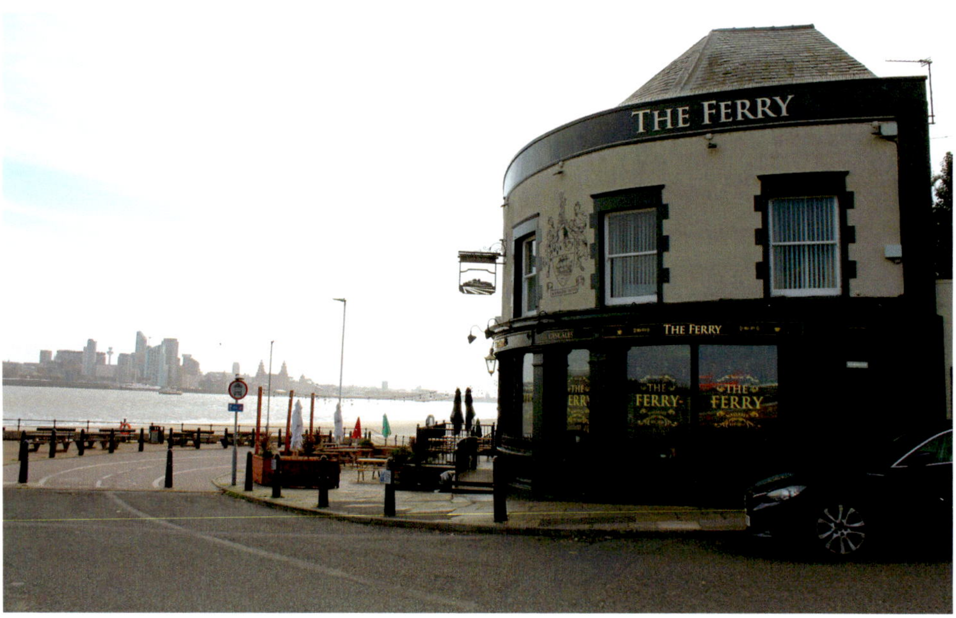

Egremont Ferry pub and the River Mersey in 2024.

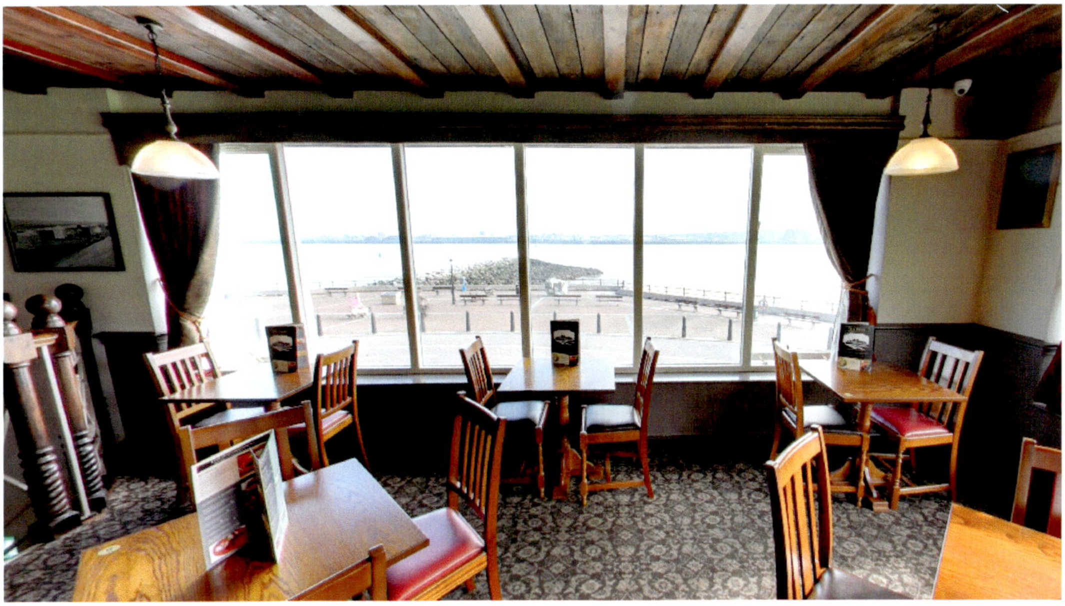

View of the River Mersey from the upstairs dining room.

The Egremont Ferry nowadays has not changed that much within, other than a marvellous dining area being provided upstairs where formerly the weight-lifting club used to practice before concerns about the ceiling falling in put a stop to it. Gone are the days when hundreds of ships and boats of all descriptions would pass by on the tides, but there are still few finer views across to Liverpool than this. As the current website states, 'The Egremont Ferry is an historic pub with unsurpassed views over the River Mersey and the iconic Liverpool skyline.'

2. The Boot Inn, Liscard

There has been a pub on the site of The Boot since the sixteenth century, being one of four hostelries mentioned in the Alehouse Register of 1561. In 1925 the present mock-Tudor building replaced a similar black and white half-timbered structure, which, although it was narrower than the current pub, was located further out into Wallasey Road and had thus become a troublesome bottleneck in the road. As was standard practice at the time, the new pub was built while the old one still stood, to enable the licence to be transferred overnight, the old one then being demolished. This inconvenient system is evidenced by other pubs in the area and would not be improved until the 1960s when common sense prevailed.

The large boot once encased in the foyer told the fabulous tale of how the pub got its name and the flowery prose is worth repeating verbatim:

> One wild dark night when all were snoring snug abed, a fierce wild horseman, bedaubed with muck and blood did gallop to the door, making a thunderous rump

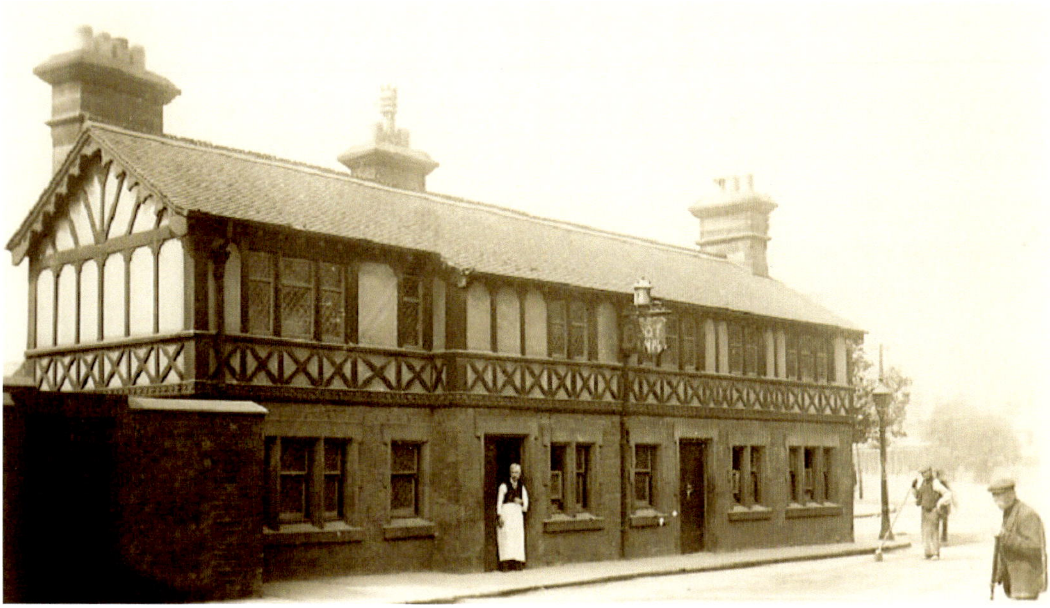

The old Boot Inn from 1910.

> thereon, when our hoaste did open unto him, he rushed into the house, a big jack boot in one hand, and a great house pistol in t'other, calling wild foul words for instant meat and drink. He had a beastly savage look, and our hoaste did eye him well while meat and drink went bolling down his wolfish maw. Thinks Jack, there's booty in that boot, for when he thumped it on the board there was a clink of gold, the pistol too was bye. Our honest Jack was cute and bold and when he brought more wine he spilt it on the man and when he turned in wrath Jack whipped the pistol to his sconce and called for his lusty wife and bucksome Joan, and they did bind the robber safe and secure, and make the gold lined boot secure. This scarce well done when three gentlemen, one with bloody sconce and bootless leg, who when he saw the robber bound was glad but soon began to wave his boot. Now our hoaste begin to bid his man bring the gold lined boot. The gentleman was then in hearty mood and gave ten guineas to our hoaste, ten more to lusty wife and bucksome Joan. He gave the robber to the gibbet and the boot to be a sign unto this inn while it doth stand.

They don't write 'em like that any more! With such a stirring story behind the name of the pub, it speaks volumes for the vacuous, imagination-free musings of the aforementioned red-braced marketeers that they dared to change the name of The Boot to the ghastly and meaningless Turnburys for a few years until common sense prevailed and they reverted to the original name. History and continuity matter when it comes to pub names.

The pub in its latest incarnation is now nearing 100 years itself and is still a very popular venue. It was one of the last pubs on Wirral to retain the bell push service

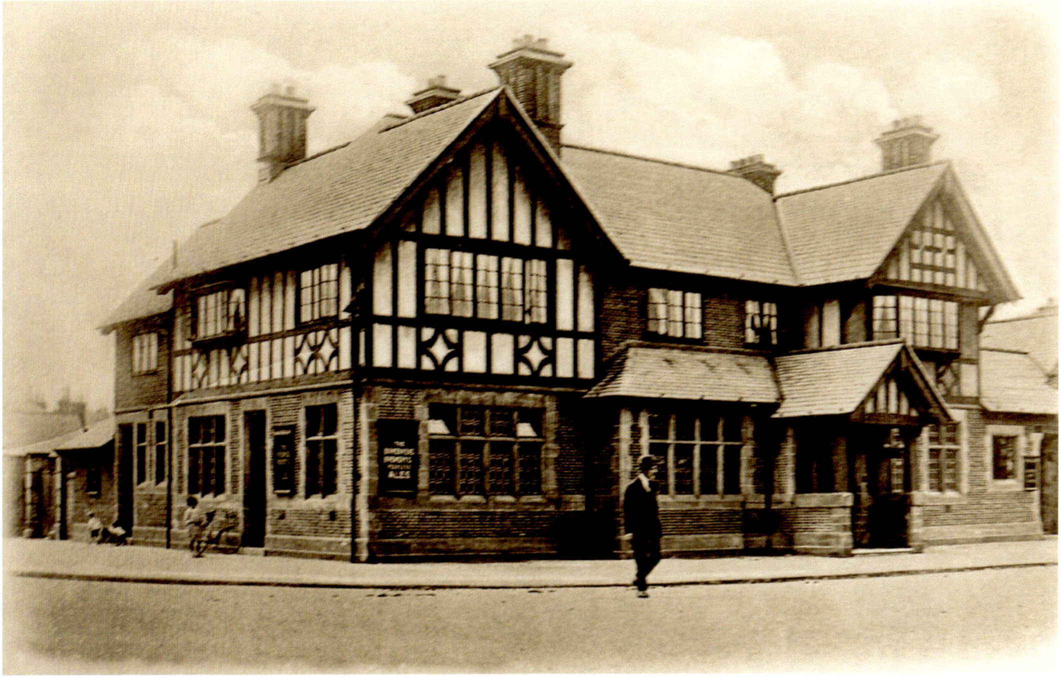

The later Boot Inn, *c*. 1950.

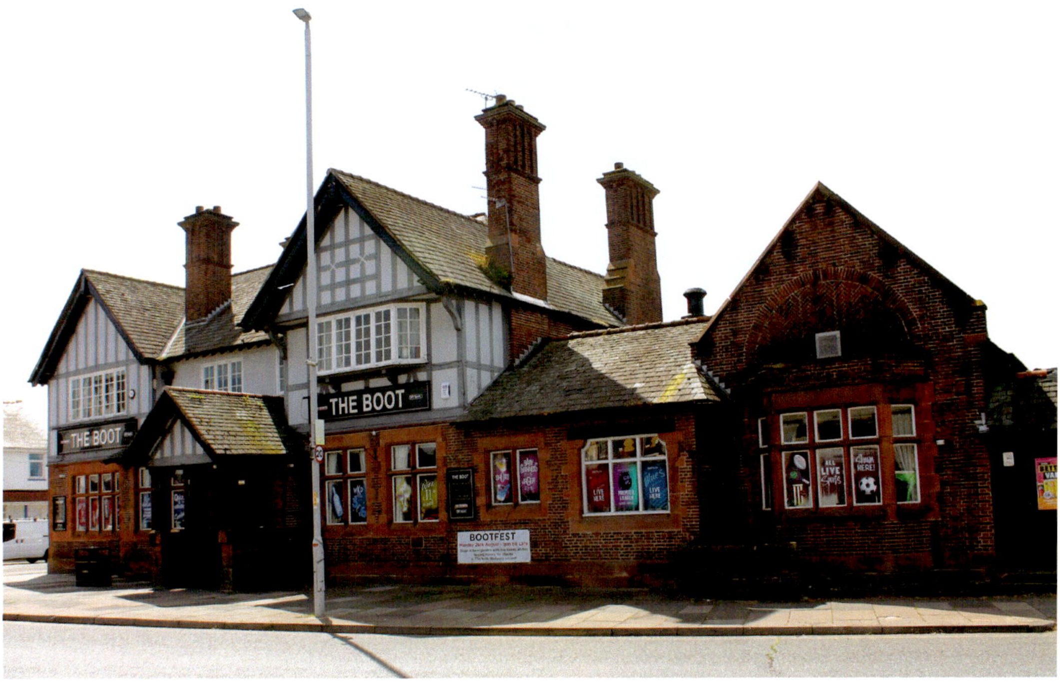

The Boot Inn in 2024.

system where you could order drinks without the inconvenience of having to go to the bar. Such bone-idleness has now been superseded by an app.

3. The Primrose, Liscard

This pub can trace its origins back to 1841 when it was listed in the local Directory of Trades as a grocery and beer shop, a common combination back in the day. It had gained a reputation over the years for its rose gardens, which were extensive and a major attraction for the pub. It was not the gardens which furnished the pub with its name however, as it was named after *The Primrose*, a paddle steamer utilised as a ferry boat on the nearby River Mersey. It was called the Primrose Tavern but was shortened when the original pub was pulled down and the current pub erected in 1923.

James Mellor and Sons were a family firm of Liverpool brewers and were responsible for remodelling the interior in conjunction with architects Prescott and Davies, who made such a fine job of the interior that CAMRA have deemed it worthy of a rating of three stars, which they class as 'a pub interior of exceptional national importance'. Praise indeed. The citation particularly praises the original wood panelling along with the broad Tudor arch, richly plastered ceiling and a good deal of attractive stained glass. Some of the original seating and bell pushes also survive. As mentioned in the introduction, original untouched fittings such as these are extremely rare.

The pub nowadays is a family friendly space, while on match days it creates a great atmosphere for local football fans with special matchday promotions, whether they support the Mighty Reds or the other smaller teams in the area. Although located somewhat off-the-beaten track between Liscard and New Brighton it is usually busy and shares its locale with another historic pub called The Saddle just a minutes walk away.

The original Primrose Inn from an old postcard, *c.* 1902.

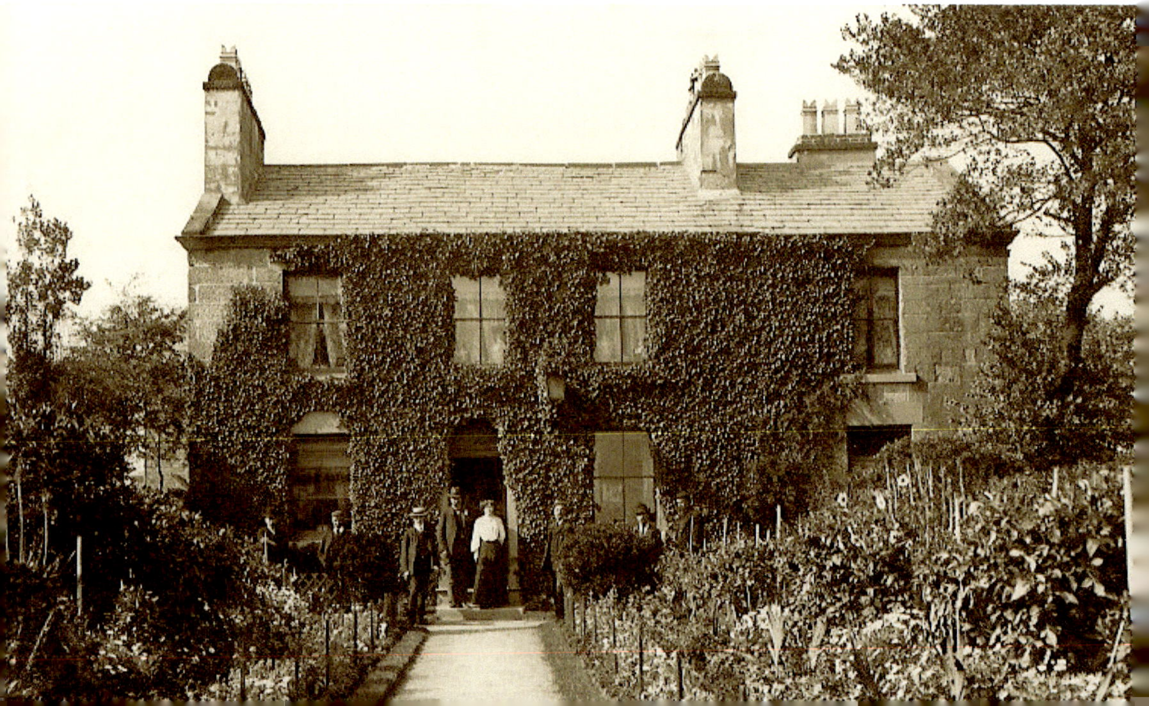

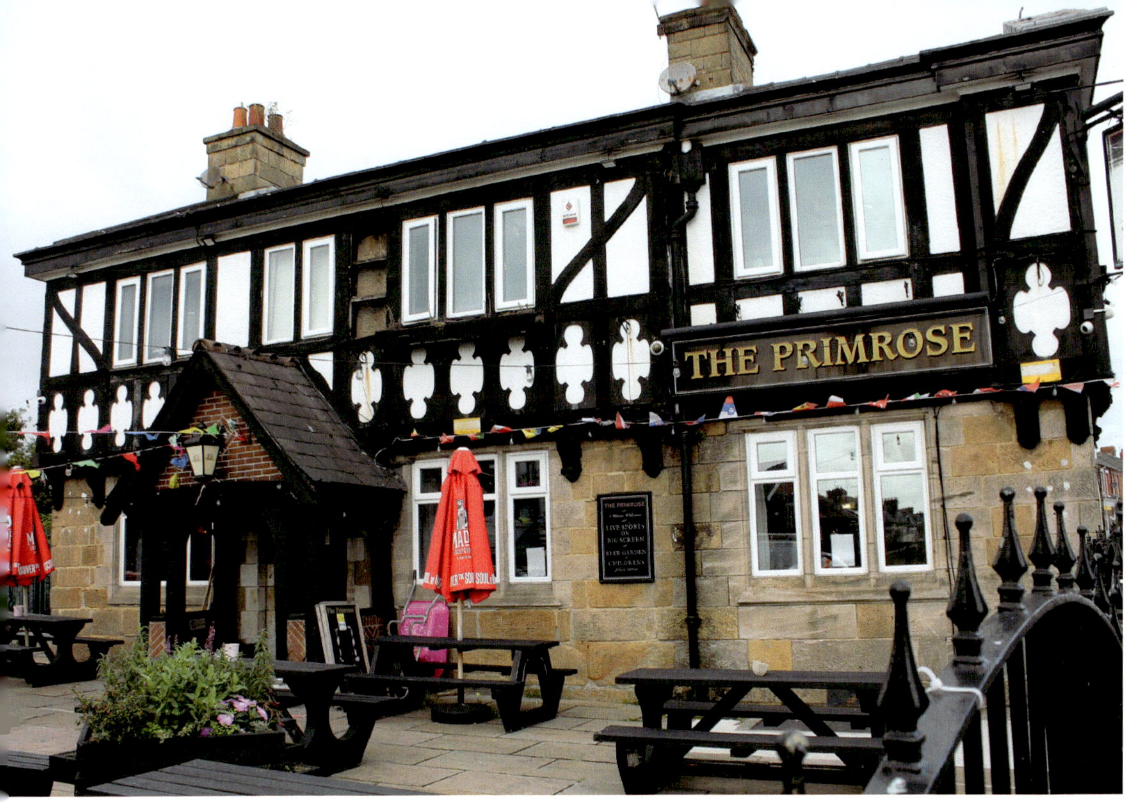

The Primrose in 2024.

4. The Magazine Hotel, New Brighton

There is something otherworldly about the area known as The Magazines. It is classed as a Conservation Area and lies adjacent to the River Mersey with a small core of historic buildings including the oddly shaped Magazine Hotel with its two full height canted bays. Dating from 1759 and built to serve a small community of fishermen, it was originally called The Black Horse but when the government decided to build a powder magazine near to the foreshore here the pub changed its name to The Magazine. Ships arriving into the port of Liverpool had to discharge their supply of gunpowder ashore during their stay, and as the original magazine was at Brownlow Hill, a heavily populated part of the city, it was deemed appropriate to risk the lives of Wirral yokels rather than the good people of Liverpool by moving their lethal cargoes over the other side of the river. It must therefore be one of the few pubs named after a potential agent of the regulars' demise.

Being next to the shoreline made the pub popular with smugglers and many a barrel of rum or sheaf of tobacco was exchanged when the revenue men were not about. This is possibly also the source for the story of hauntings at the pub which would have kept the inquisitive (nosey) people away from the area when contraband was being moved, rather like a storyline from Scoobie Doo. Persistent stories of strange goings on may or may not be related to this ruse but the story goes that the ghost of a witch which turfed people violently out of their beds or brought serious bad luck was the spirit of an old woman who was wrongly convicted of witchcraft. She is said to have tried to

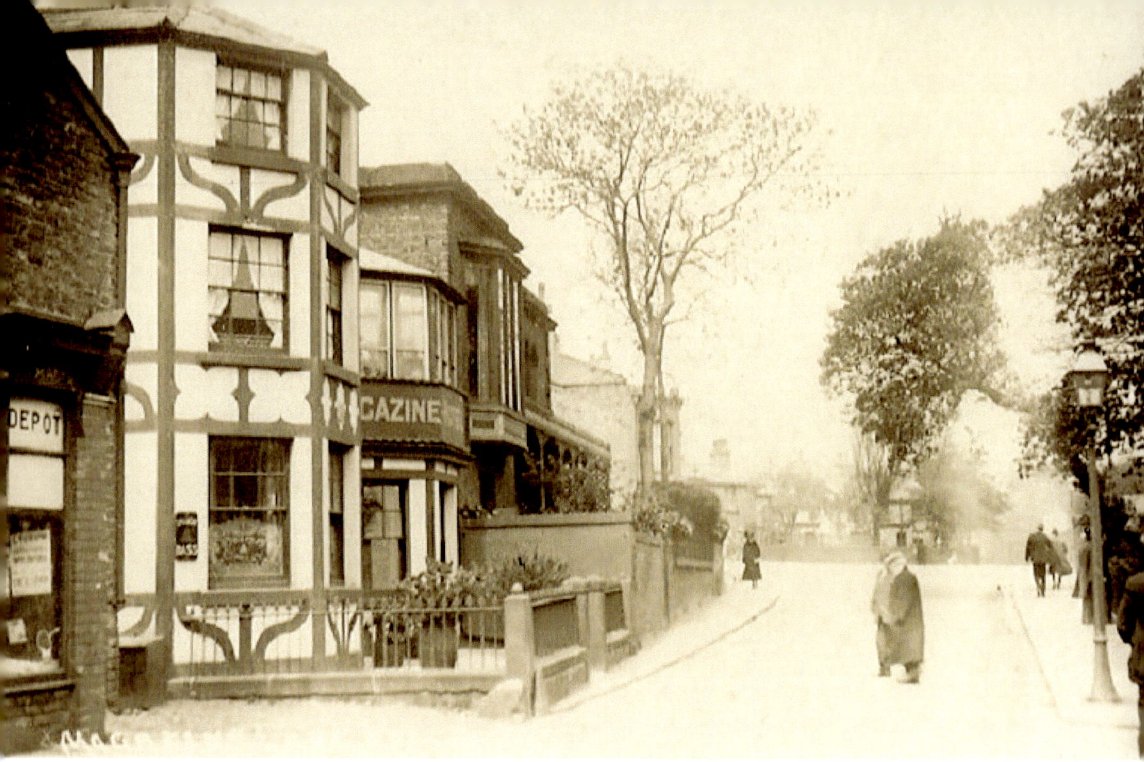

Above: The Magazine from Magazine Brow in 1905.

Below: The Magazine in 2024.

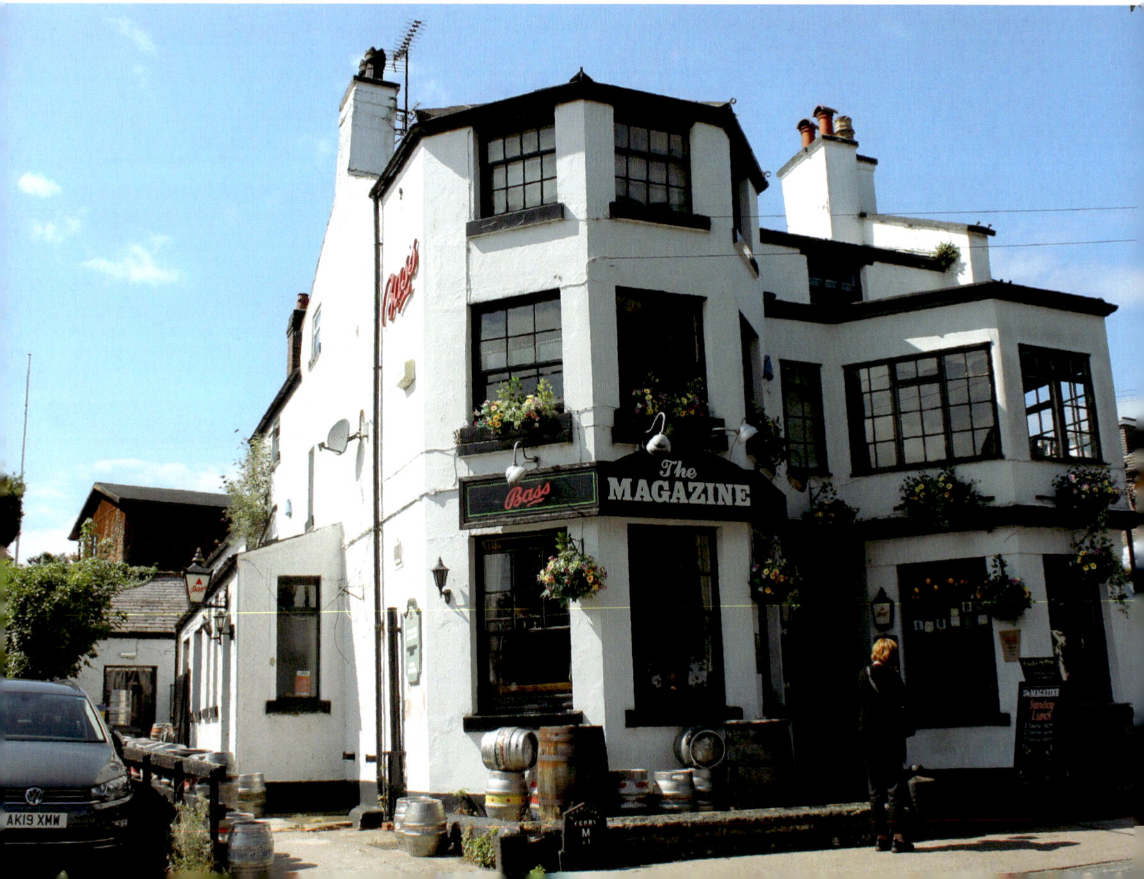

kill one of the ancestors of her accusers on a boat in the Mersey, and tried to throttle another when they had retired to The Magazine for the night. An effigy of the witch had hung in the pub for many years and serious harm had come to anyone foolish enough to meddle with this spooky relic. When someone had the temerity to actually steal the effigy in 2010 there followed a serious fire when the pub nearly burnt down. Coincidence or paranormal arson, you decide.

The pub was listed in Bagshaws 1850 Directory. When renamed it came into the ownership of the Argyle Brewery before being taken over by Birkenhead Brewery (they of the Peerless Ales) before becoming a Bass House, which it remains to this day. There are multiple small rooms and a larger bar area along with an excellent outside area with attendant bowling green, a facility that many pubs had in the past but few retain today. The Magazine Bowling Club was founded way back in 1853 incidentally. There are many retained Victorian fixtures and fittings including tiling, panelling and a sign stating 'Gentlemen Only' in the main room, which may or may not date from this time.

If you are in the vicinity do not pass up the chance to visit this fine historic pub, and a brief stroll around the surrounding area should also prove rewarding.

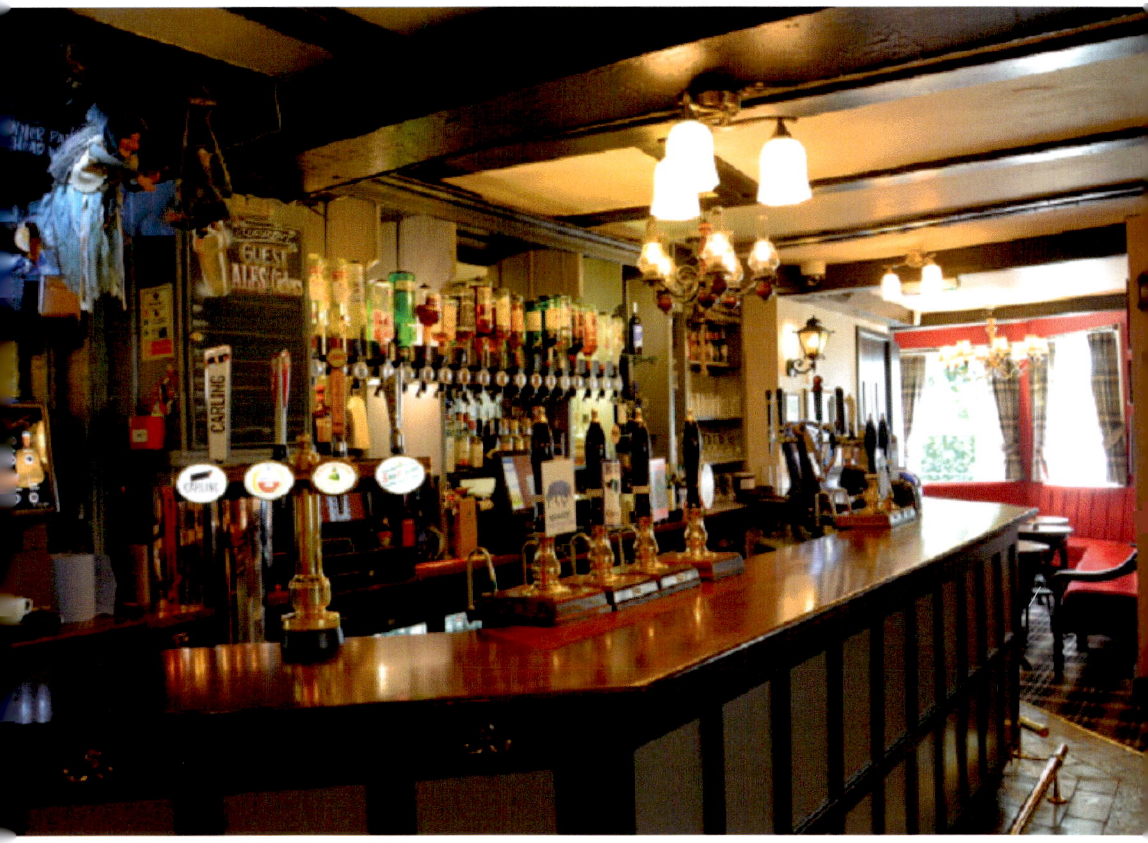

The main bar at the Magazine.

5. The Cheshire Cheese, Wallasey Village

The Alehouse Register of 1561 contained 'the names of all persons which kept alehouses within the Hundred of Wirral' Its yellowing pages make for interesting reading, with the entry covering Wallasey showing the names of just four ale houses, only two of which remain, albeit not in the original buildings. They were The Pool Inn in Poulton, The Seacombe Ferry, The Boot in Liscard and The Cheshire Cheese in Wallasey Village. The original 'Cheese' was a tiny, thatched cottage at the foot of Folly Lane opposite School Lane, with small windows, worn steps and an old pub sign attached to the chimney.

It was described in Philip Sulley's 1889 book 'The Hundred of Wirral' as 'ancient and picturesque' but it could not have been the most comfortable of places to enjoy a drink. A secret passage was alleged to have existed under the pub, which led up to the nearby St Hilary's Church but this seems extremely unlikely and no trace of it has been found to date. It has also been claimed with rather more conviction that Charles II and William III both stayed at the old Cheshire Cheese, the latter on his way over to Ireland and the Battle of the Boyne. Prince George of Denmark and the Duke of Ormond apparently also popped in for a swift half in 1690.

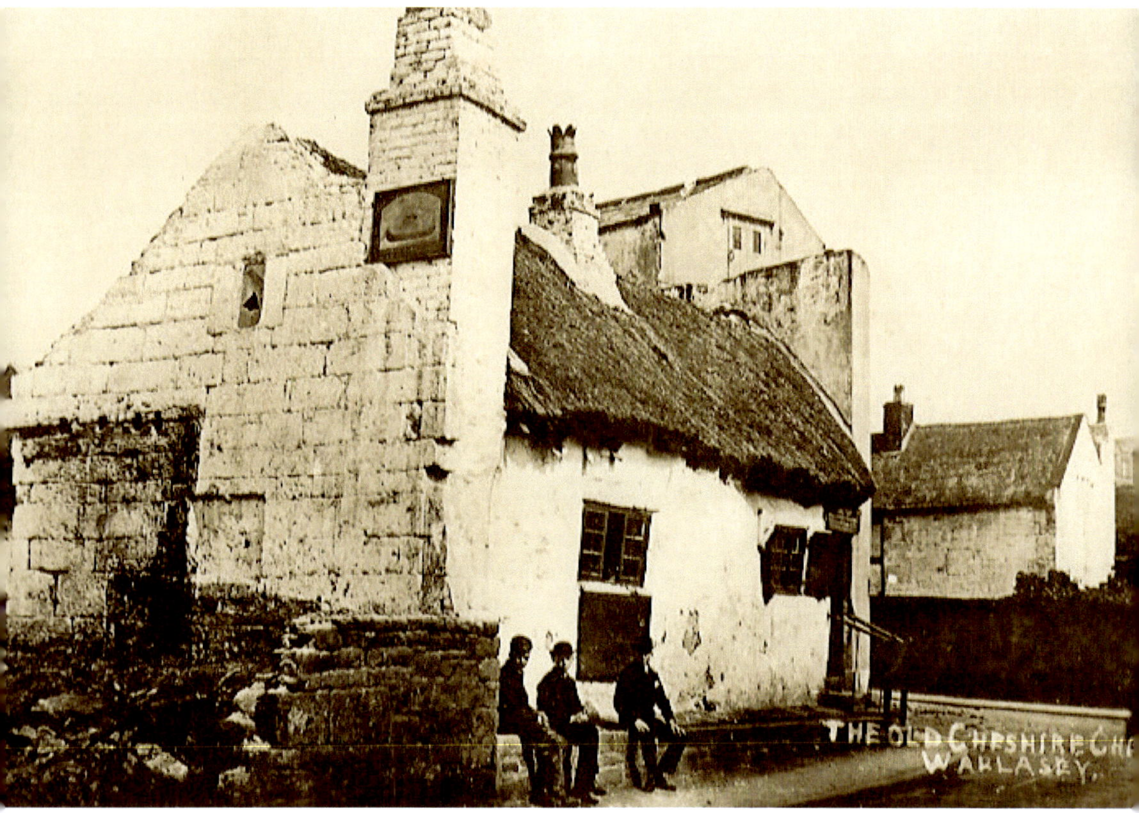

The original Cheshire Cheese pub, *c*. 1870.

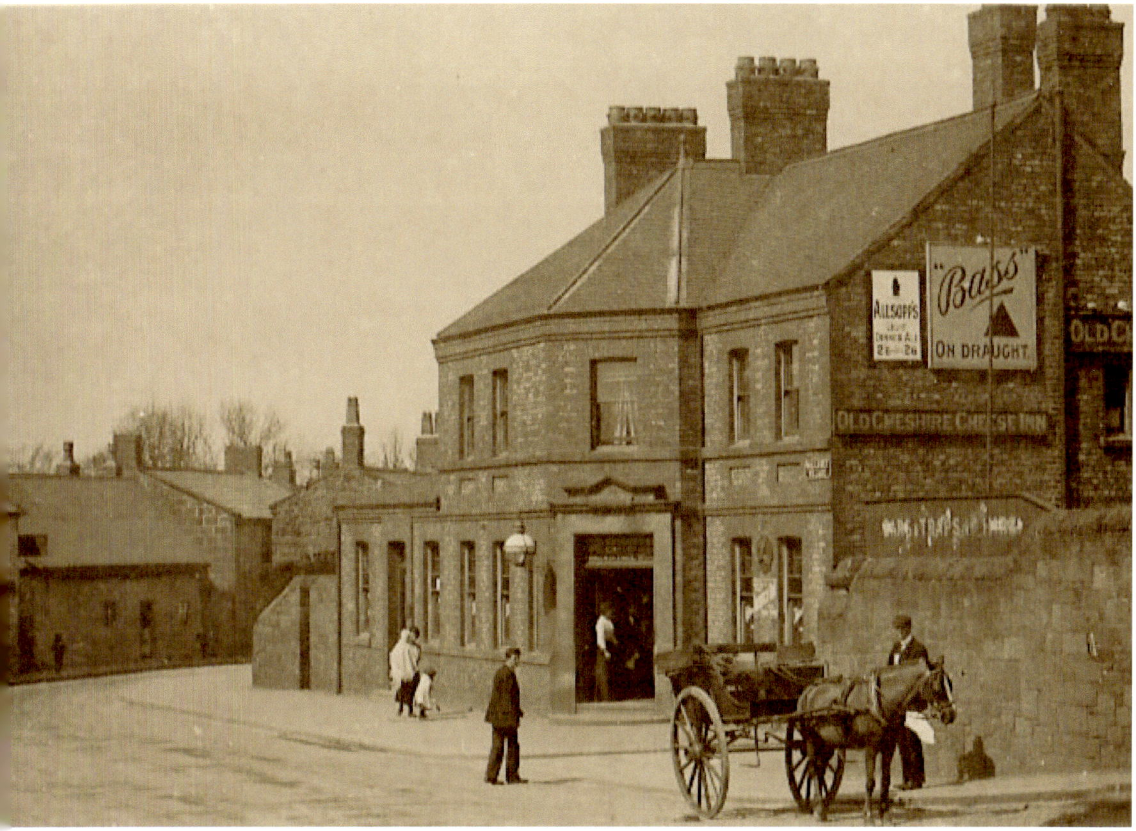

A postcard view of the newly built Cheshire Cheese.

There were a few other choices of pub as The Black Horse, The Ring O'Bells and The Sebastopol Inn were all within a minutes walking distance of the Cheese. Spraggs Brewery was also just around the corner at the top of Leasowe Road and they supplied their beer to most of the pubs in the area. All of these hostelries were swept away when the road from Poulton to Wallasey Village was widened to allow for the laying of tramlines and the Cheshire Cheese was pulled down and the current building erected in 1885 with Higsons taking over the supply of beer in 1919 when Spraggs closed down. The new pub was instantly popular with the locals as it was far bigger, with many small intimate rooms along with a larger bar area. It continues to be a regular haunt for lovers of real ales, especially as an area has been set aside at the side of the pub for real ale festivals, with lovers of gin also being catered for with a large selection of gins and other spirits to tantalise the tastebuds. The Ship Inn on Breck Road was demolished in 2022, which leaves just The Cheshire Cheese, The Farmers Arms, The Lighthouse and The Black Horse (Sheridans) as the only pubs in the area, although the recently refurbished Nelson (The Big Nelly) in Grove Road is well worth a visit.

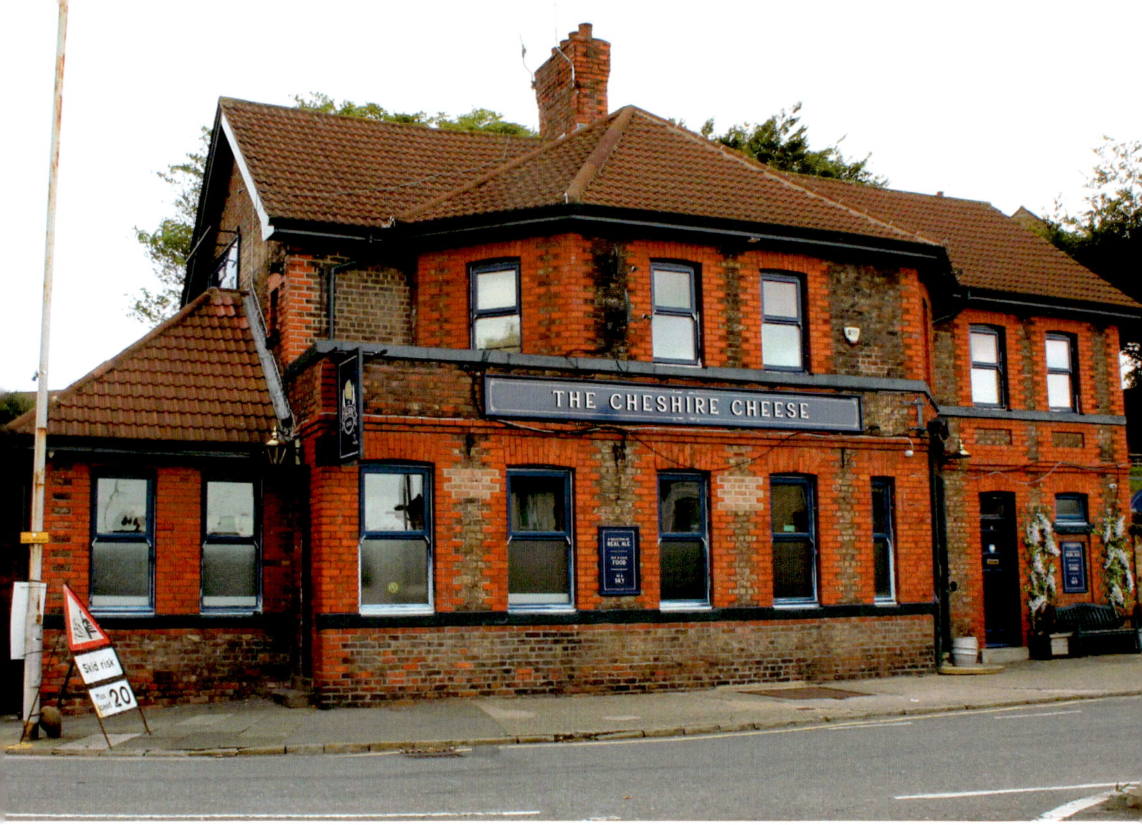

The Cheshire Cheese in 2024.

6. The Coach and Horses, Moreton

The first mention of a Coach and Horses pub in Moreton was around 1685 by a local man who visited a race meeting on nearby Moreton shore, a venue that would become the forerunner of the Grand National incidentally. Having had a successful day gambling on the horses he had retired to the Coach and Horses to spend some of his winnings. The building was part of a row of cottages beside a narrow country lane, which led through to Meols and Hoylake. It was one of three inns in the area, all of a similar size and all fated to be demolished and replaced by more modern versions, although each kept its original name. The Farmers Arms was located at the back of the Coach and Horses and what was known as the Plough Inn and Druids Arms was located where a Tesco outlet now stands.

The first known tenant was Jack Tarrant, but the most renowned was Sylvester Samuel Morris, known as Old Sam and apparently quite a character. He was landlord from 1915 until 1931 and strictly old school – no drunkenness or rowdiness under his watch – with a penchant for forcefully ejecting miscreants who did not follow his house rules. It was during his tenancy that Bents Brewery took over the Coach and Horses and it later became a Birkenhead Brewery House. They took the decision to demolish it and build a much larger pub to cater for the rapidly expanding population of Moreton and Leasowe. As was the case with all pubs at the time, the old pub was left standing whilst the new one was being built (see The Boot

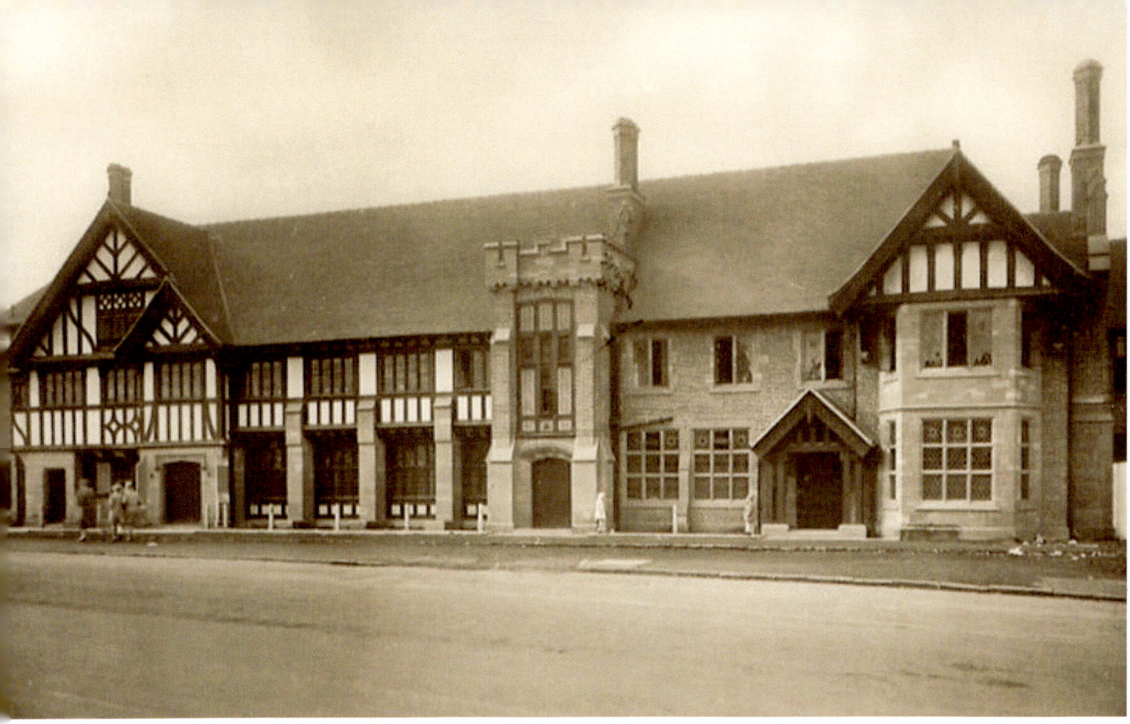

The Coach and Horses in Moreton, *c.* 1948.

Inn). The difference in size was manifest as the huge new pub was created behind the old one, the licence being transferred overnight in February 1928 and the original inn being demolished soon afterwards. The site now forms part of the service road outside the new pub. Coins dating back to 1791 were discovered in the foundations of the old inn.

Several books have referred to the new pub as The Cathedral due to its enormous size but I have not come across any local people calling it by that nickname. They refer to it merely as The Big House. Nevertheless, it is a huge edifice with a vast function room upstairs. A large back door originally gave access to the rear of the pub, which had a bath room, a facility much appreciated by the locals, most of whom would not have had access to a proper bath at home. 3*d* in old money would have bought you a nice relaxing soak. This handy facility would later become an off-licence. Such was its size that an entire mock street was created inside the pub in the 1980s when Berni Inns opened one of their popular restaurants here. The street had individual houses set up for diners to enjoy their meals (prawn cocktail, steak and chips followed by Black Forest gateau was *de rigueur*). It was a strange but rewarding experience, made rather poignant by the fact that a row of genuine shops had been demolished to create this artificial row of shops!

An old advertisement for the Coach and Horses ran 'Catering for large and small parties on the shortest notice. The Best of everything at the lowest possible price'. Nowadays most advertising for functions at the pub are done through Facebook and Twitter, etc., but it remains a popular venue for the socially minded and fun-loving people of Wirral.

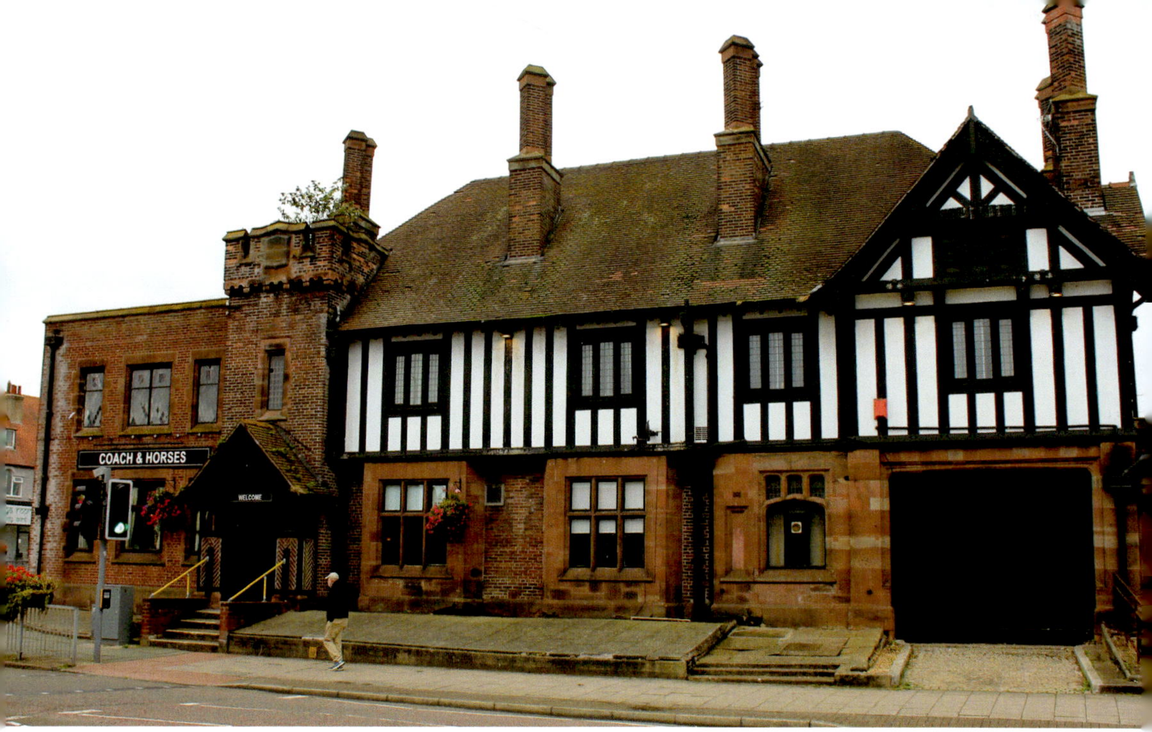

The Coach and Horses from Pasture Road.

7. The Stork, Birkenhead

The Stork Hotel in Price Street, Birkenhead, is one of the most complete and unaltered pubs in Wirral. Ruth Goodman, the well-known historian of all things Victorian, in her book *How to be a Victorian* in the section on Victorian pubs she spoke of urban examples from the 1840s to the 1860s being 'grand, veritable palaces of the people'. She singled out The Stork as 'the finest example of such a pub I have ever patronised ... not far from the park that sought to entice people away from such a culture'. She continued: 'Exuberant decoration runs everywhere: in the frosted glass, the patterned tiling on the floor and walls, the wallpaper and even the plaster on the ceiling'.

Ironically, however, most of the details of the pub stem from an Edwardian remodelling of 1903 rather than the Victorian period and begin with the marvellous glazed brick and tile frontage including colourful blue pilasters, which whets the appetite for the delights within. And the interior certainly doesn't disappoint. The inner lobby has a door with 'Bar' etched in a full height partition, which also boasts etched, stained and leaded glass panels. The narrow corridor running round the bar has a splendid mosaiced floor, which was only rediscovered in 2000 for the first time in decades.

The turquoise theme is continued in a dado at the servery and other walls, many containing Art Nouveau patterns in yellow, orange and blue. The abundance of blue within the design was due to it being the owners Threlfall's house colours. It transpires that the tiling for the Stork was by George Swift and Co. of the Swan Tile Works in Liverpool, home of the Liver Birds, a veritable ornithological jamboree. In addition, there is an original fireplace in the corridor with a beautiful mahogany surround and brown glazed brick interior.

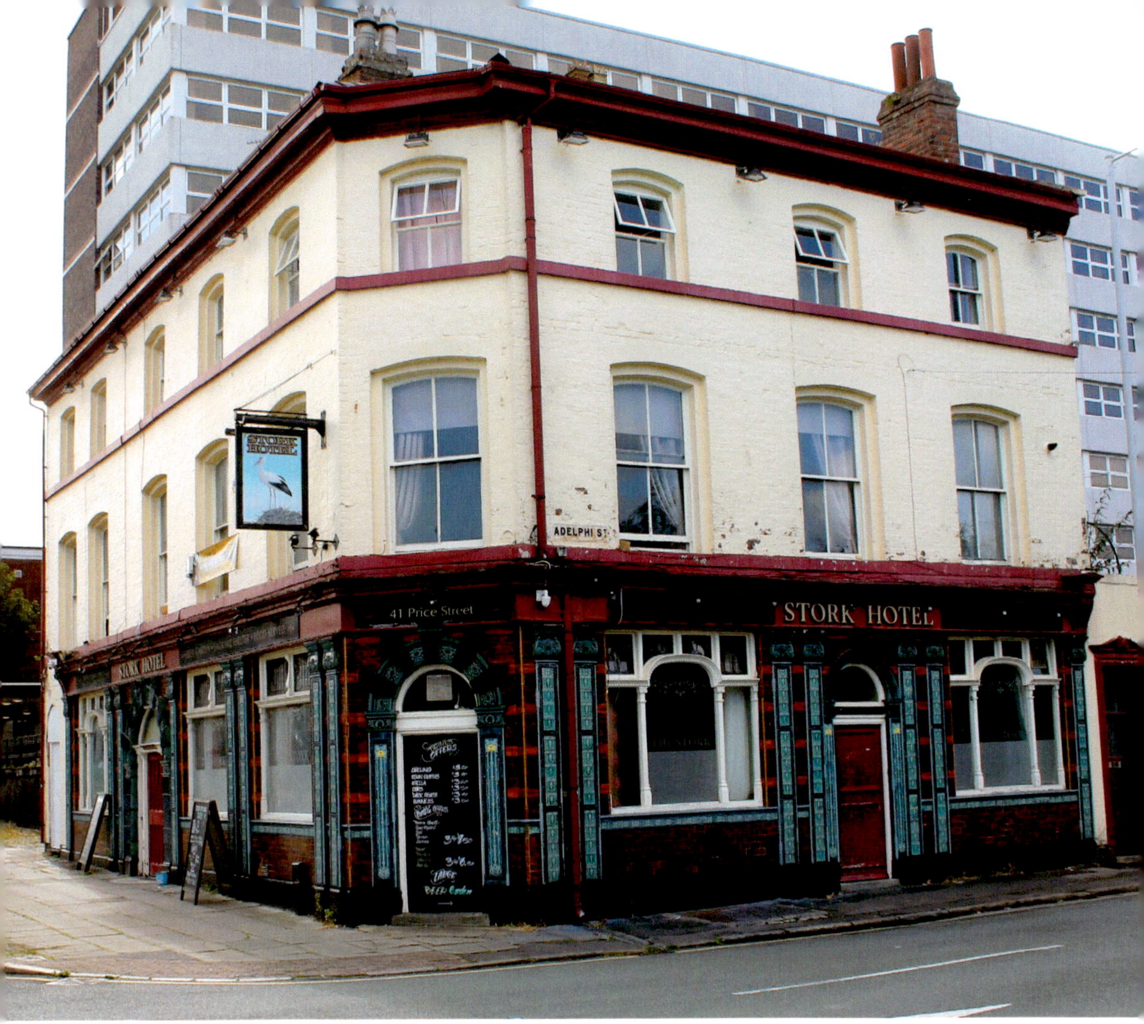

Above: Corridor at the Stork with serving hatch.

Right: Detail of outside decoration at the Stork.

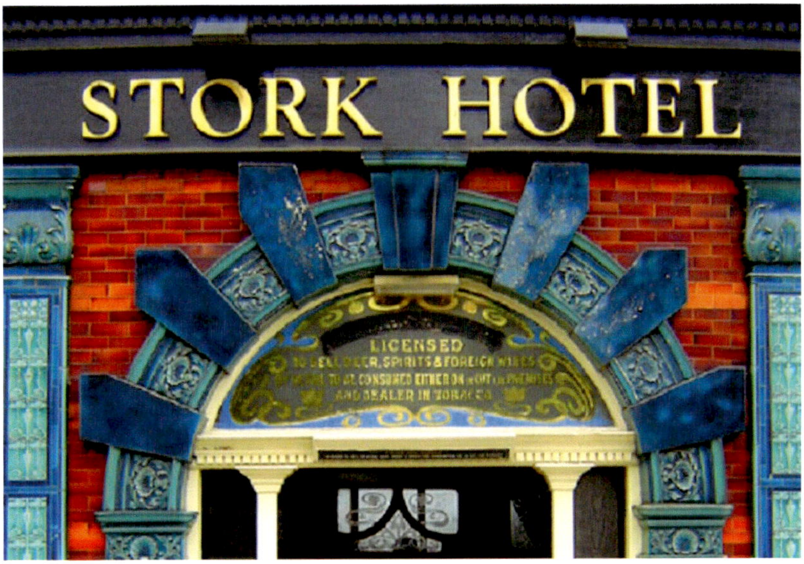

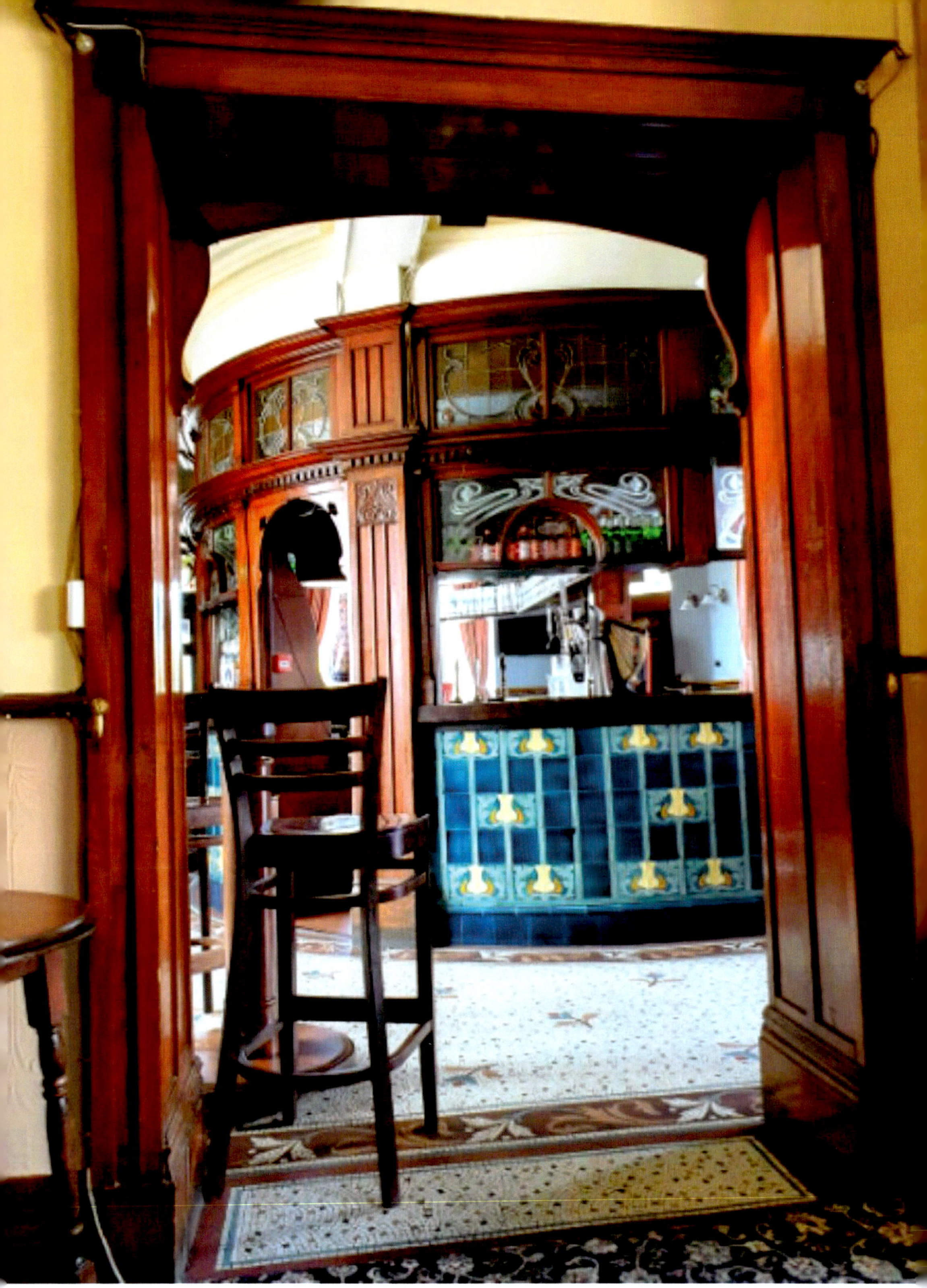

The main bar showing tiling and glasswork.

It just goes on and on: original bell pushes, more mosaic floored passageways, more frosted glass and tiling everywhere. It is such an assault on the senses that one needs to sit down and have a pint, real ale of course in respect to the surroundings. It is quite easy to forget as you sit contentedly supping your pint that you are in downtown Birkenhead. It is easy to understand why so many working men (and it was only men at this time) would want to spend so much time in the pub as it would have been preferable to returning home to a cold and colourless tenement or tiny terraced house. Which of course is why the breweries went to such expense to make their pubs so appealing. And they had plenty of choice in hostelries in this area with practically a pub on every corner; The New Inn, The Cleveland, The Boars Head, The Angel and The Arab Arms were all but a minute's walk away. Pub crawls tended to be very local affairs in those days but with more and more pubs closing, more inventive drinkers developed the Astronauts Walk, which began at The Globe and took in The Comet, The North Star and The Rising Sun before, as all good astronauts do, ending up in The Pacific. Simple pleasures.

8. Gallaghers, Birkenhead

This is the latest incarnation on this site, just a stone's throw from Woodside Ferry and the River Mersey, built at this location to catch the passing trade from the ferries, as well as the nearby Woodside railway station. Built in 1826, it began life as The Prince of Denmark, changing its name to The Hamlet in the 1850s. Those of you who know your Shakespeare will know that Hamlet was indeed The Prince of Denmark before coming to a sticky end in Act V. It had another name change in the 1980s when it became The Chester Arms after the pubs address in Chester Street and again when Cains took over the pub, being called The Dispensary before being renamed yet again, this time by the new owners Frank and Sue Gallagher.

Frank and Sue were barbers by trade and already owned a barber's shop in nearby Market Street, but it was a bit of a left field decision to set up another barber's shop within the pub itself. It seemed to work, however, and the unusual combination of pub and barber's shop certainly created a buzz (no pun intended) – always a good thing in the hospitality trade. The *Liverpool Echo* took note and ran an article headed 'Unique pub is a cut above the rest'. Hilarious copy. The barber's shop is no longer there, however, as it was decided to close it in 2016 to create more room for customers of the pub, although a reminder remains in the form of a red and white pole to the left of the bar.

Looking at the pub from the street, it is not apparent quite how big it is, as the front is narrow but goes back through the long bar, along a narrow corridor and out into a linear beer garden at the back. The interior is crammed full of the usual paraphernalia, mainly shipping memorabilia and militaria, including a collection of drums and military tunics and poppies painted on the ceiling. There is a function room upstairs and a handsome leaded glass skylight to illuminate proceedings. The final point of interest, however, is to be found outside where a large mural has been created by local artist Paul Curtis. It depicts the legend of the Birkenhead Drill where the cry of 'Women and children first' became the adopted code for those on board a sinking ship. The *Birkenhead* sank on 26 February 1852, and the full story of the tragedy is outlined

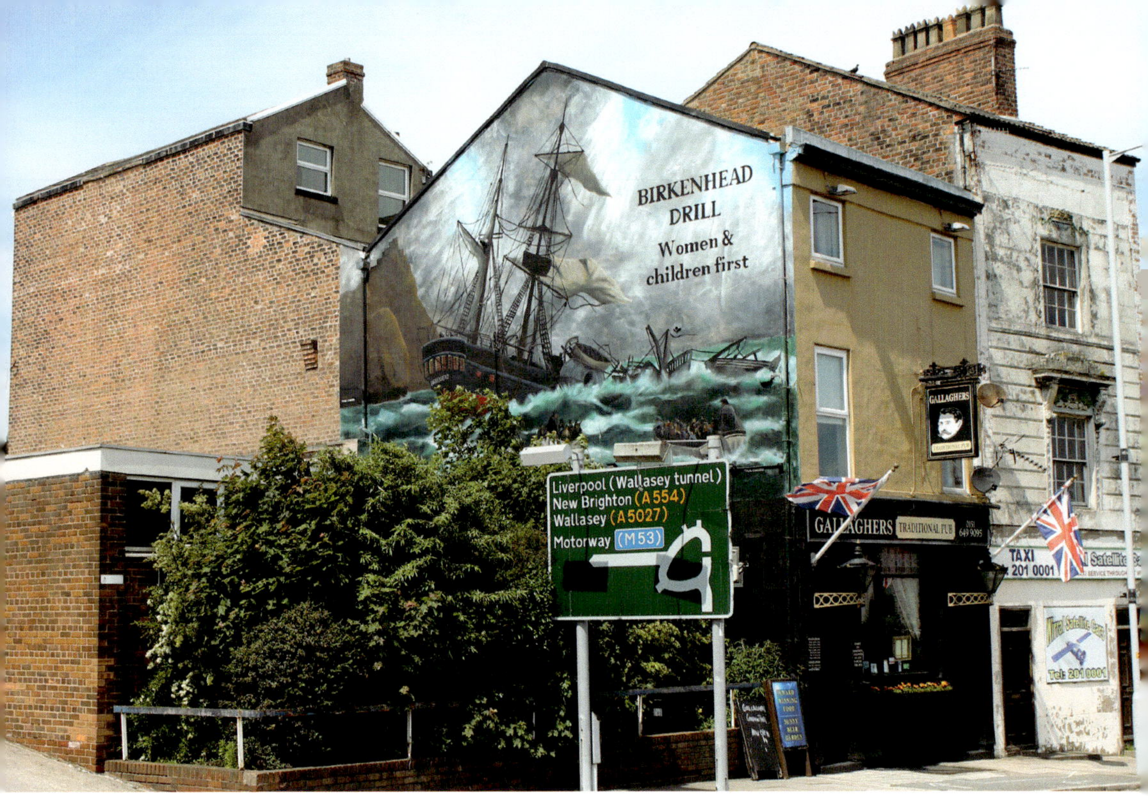

Above: Gallaghers.

Below: Gallaghers pub when it was known as The Hamlet.

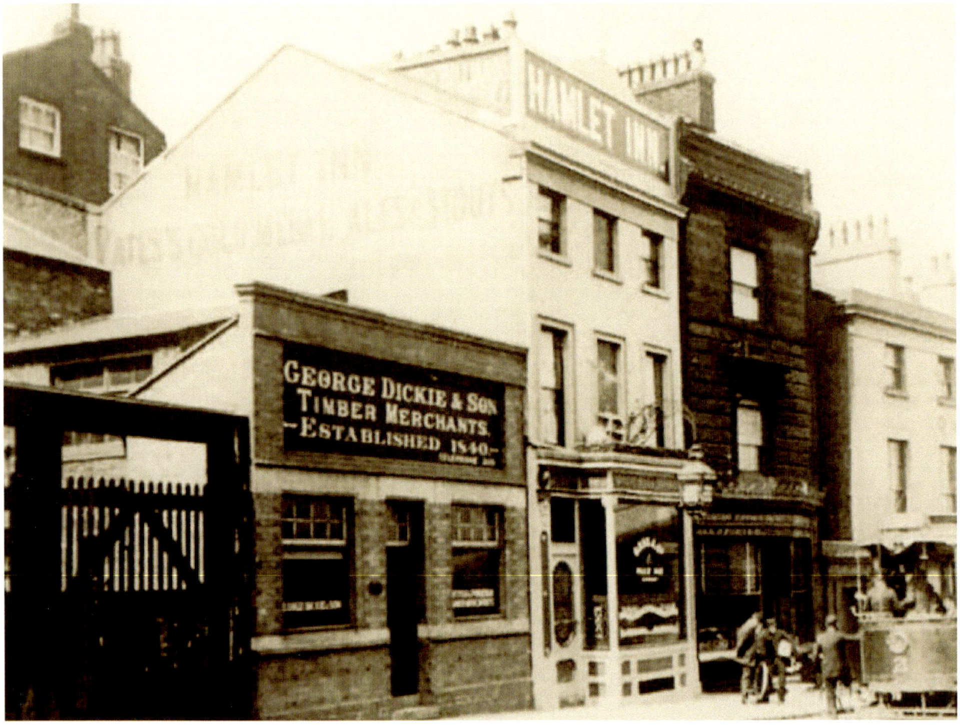

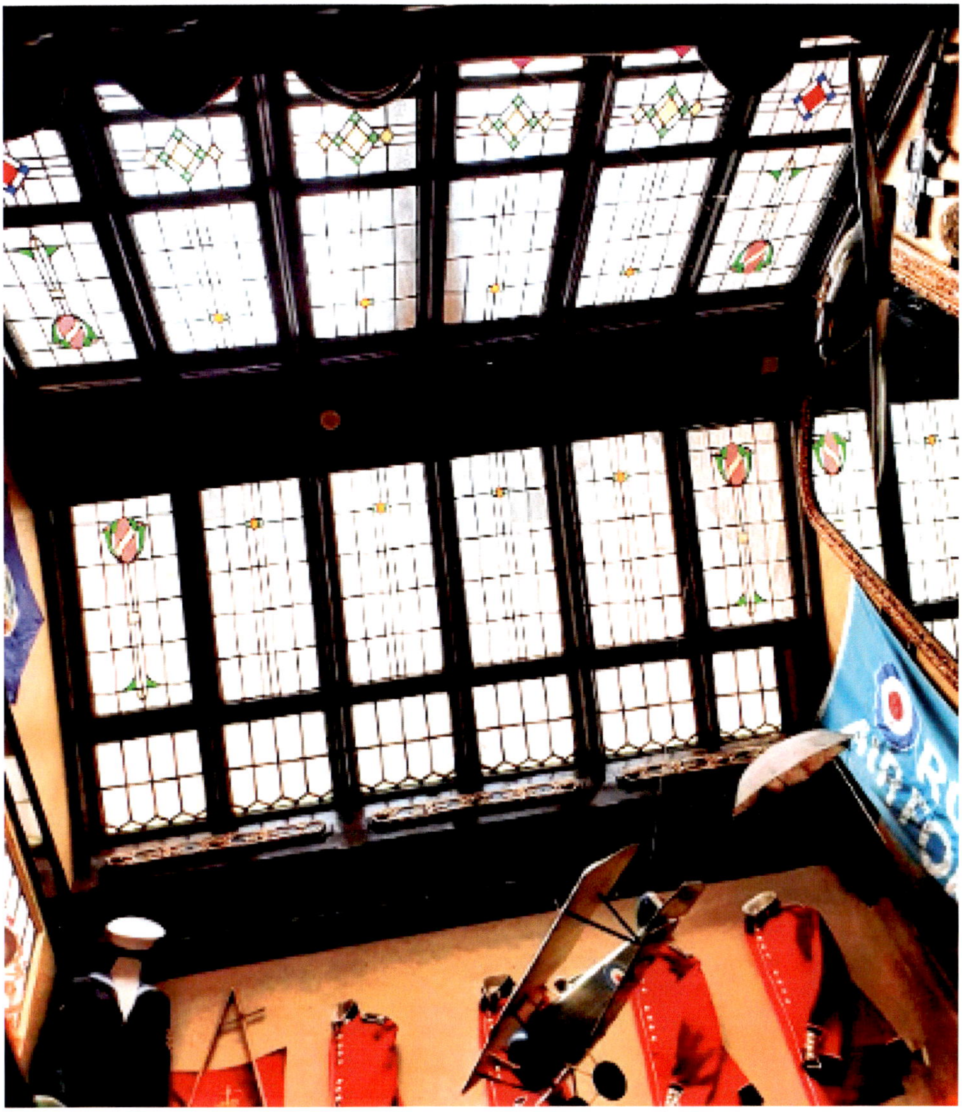

The upstairs skylight at Gallaghers.

in a picture frame in the pub. The heroism of the men on board, soldiers rather than sailors incidentally, runs thus: 'The ranks of troops stood fast. Not one man tried to save himself. As if on cue The Birkenhead gave an almighty shudder and the sea started to wash right over the deck. Still the soldiers stood firm, heads held high, as they prepared themselves to make their final sacrifice'. Paul's original effort was washed off in bad weather and he was forced to start again, but managed to finish it in time for the anniversary of the sinking. Gallaghers has been voted CAMRA pub of the year on several occasions and boasts a range of constantly changing real ales, along with annual favourites such as trips to Cartmel Races and the yearly conker tournament.

9. The Queens Arms, Oxton

Up until the beginning of the nineteenth century Oxton had been an extremely poor area of Wirral, strewn with low farmers cottages and squatters' hovels. In fact it was one of the meanest parts of the entire peninsula. All this began to change, however, when the businessmen of Liverpool began to look at the elevated situation of the village, and the potential for making it a suitable place to retire to after the rigours of a day in the grimy, smoke-filled city. Being raised above the surrounding countryside had many advantages and the burgesses of the city went for it in a big way, building large houses and villas across the parish and sweeping away the worst examples of housing that spoilt their view. Limited infrastructure was needed to support these villas as most of the owners could travel into town or have their requirements fulfilled by local traders who would deliver to the houses. A small village centre, however, was created around Village Road and Rose Mount and three pubs were built, two of which survive in their original form. The Talbot was pulled down and rebuilt in a meritless 1970s style but the Shrewsbury Arms and The Queens Arms remain as built.

The Queens Arms benefits from its location on a corner site between Storeton Road and Rose Mount and was originally called 'The Queens Arms Hotel of Oxton Hill'. It was soon shortened to its current name by the pubs owner, one Thomas Hughes. His name has come down to us through nearby Hughes Lane, which has remained a narrow, unadopted lane leading around the back of the pub into Arno Road. Newburns Lane to the north of the Queens Arms contains a row of small cottages that survived the Victorian

The Queens from an old postcard of 1902.

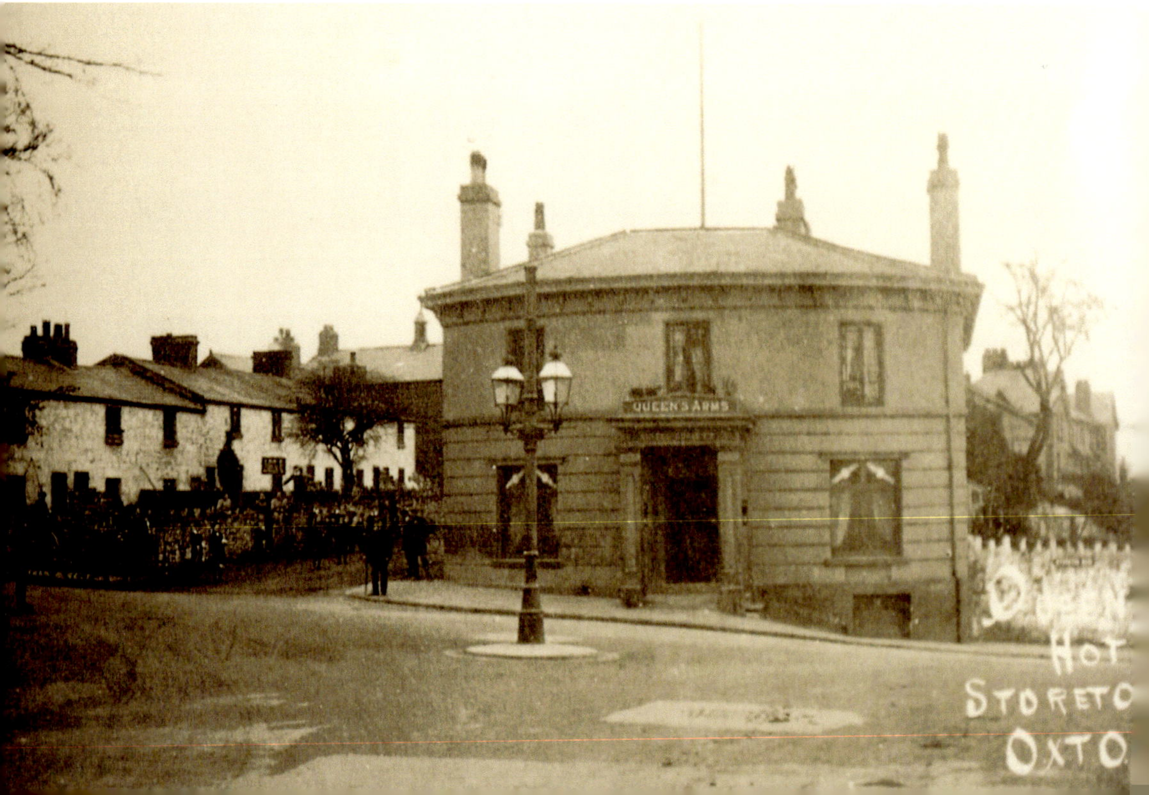

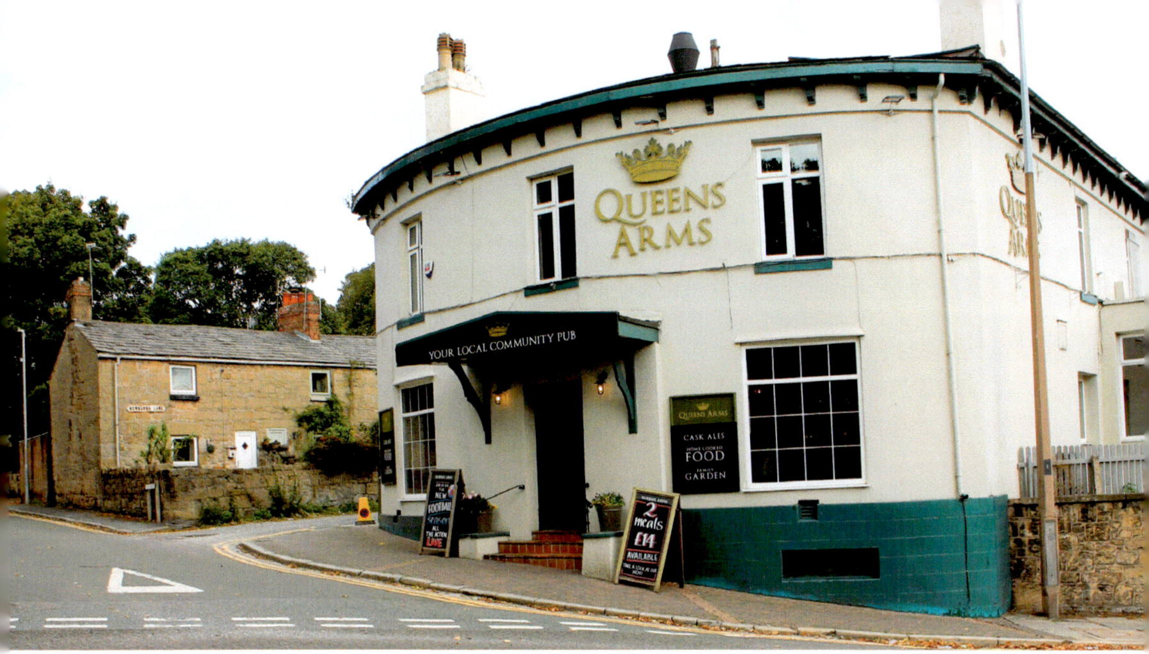

Above: The Queens and Newburns Lane.

Below: Old advertisement for The Queens Hotel, *c.* 1870.

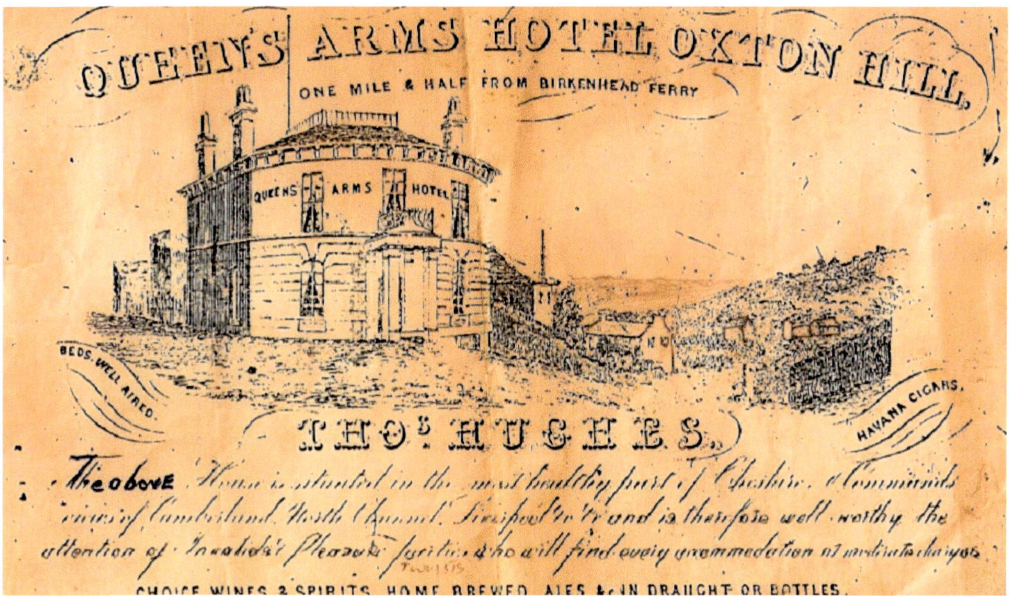

gentrification of Oxton. These cottages housed workers from the nearby Arno quarry, which provided stone for many of the buildings in the village. It would be nice to think that workers from the cottages had used stone from the Arno to build their very own local. Mr Newburn incidentally was the owner of the quarry. When constructed The Queens Arms had a nearby rival for its thirsty clientele in a beer house located in Birch Road in a cluster of simple cottages. The beer house survives but is now used as a beauty salon.

A contemporary advertisement from the *Birkenhead Advertiser* ran: 'The Queens Arms in Oxton is situated in the most healthy part of Cheshire and commands views of Cumberland, North Channel Liverpool, etc., and is therefore well worthy of the attention of invalids and pleasure parties, who will find every accommodation at moderate charges. Choice wines and spirits, home-brewed ales in draught or bottles, good stabling and lock-up coach houses. Beds well aired, Havana cigars'. Nowadays the pub has a reputation for its fine food, quiz nights and sporting events, predominantly football. The fine views may be a little more difficult to obtain but the pub remains a popular venue for locals and visitors alike.

10. The Shrewsbury Arms, Oxton

The Shrewsbury Arms is the oldest pub in Oxton, just pipping The Queens Arms to the title as it received its drinking licence a couple of months previously. The building itself, however, is older than this and was originally built as a workers cottage. This was subsequently divided into two separate cottages, the cottage bordering Claughton Firs becoming a pub in 1870. Soon after this, in 1874, the two halves were again united when the licensed premises were extended back into the original cottage, creating The Shrewsbury Arms that we know and love today.

Named after Oxton's most famous landlord, the Earl of Shrewsbury, the Talbots have owned much of the land in this area since 1521 when the 4th Earl became

Opposite: Stained glass in the porch of the Shrewsbury Arms.

Below: The Shrewsbury Arms in 2024.

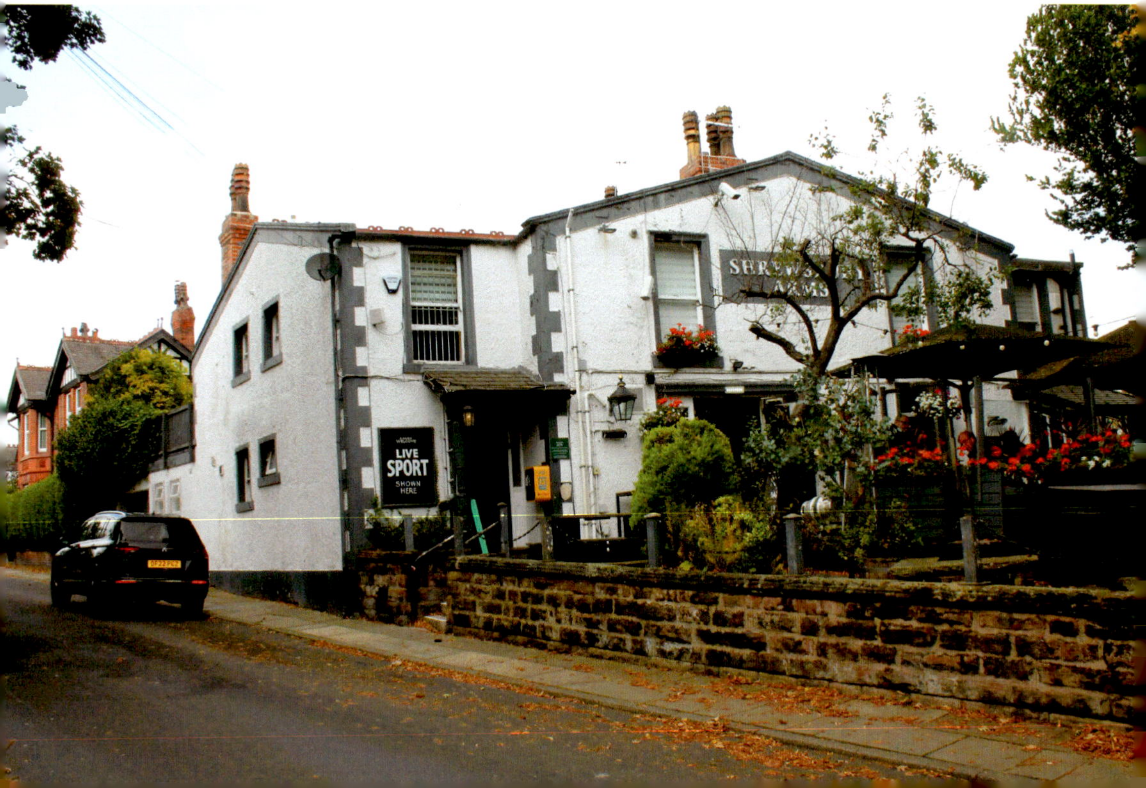

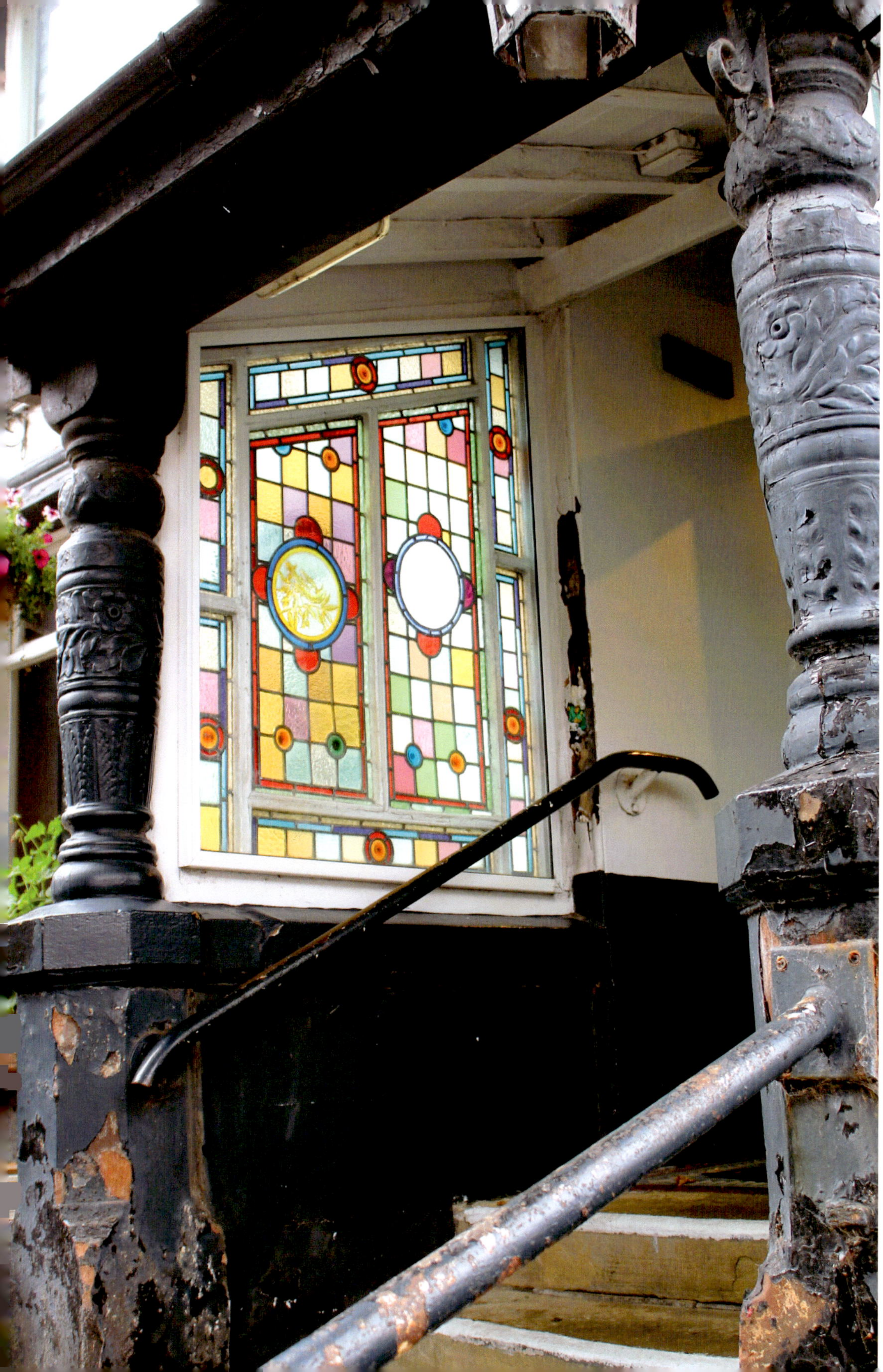

landowner, with subsequent earls inheriting the land right up until 1990 when the 22nd Earl finally relinquished the manorial title. The canny 4th Earl set up a system of restrictive building leases which in later years meant that anyone wishing to build property in Oxton had to meet certain standards of construction. When one steps into the pub it is interesting to try and work out the original format of the place as there are beams, thick walls and all manner of nooks and crannies to explore. There are some good examples of stained glass in the Claughton Firs end, always a welcome addition in any pub.

The pub occupies one of the highest points in Oxton and views over to Liverpool can still be achieved, although not as open as when the Liverpool shipowners built their fine villas, many with belvedere towers to watch out for their vessels as they steamed into port. This part of the village has thankfully been largely spared the attentions of the Philistines of the 1960s and 1970s and their unsympathetic infill, which was largely brought to an end when the major part of Oxton became a Conservation Area in April 1979, with The Shrew being right in the centre. This advantage comes into its own during the annual Secret Gardens event when many local residents open up their fine gardens to the general public and the pub becomes a hub for weary garden lovers looking for a sandwich and a drink.

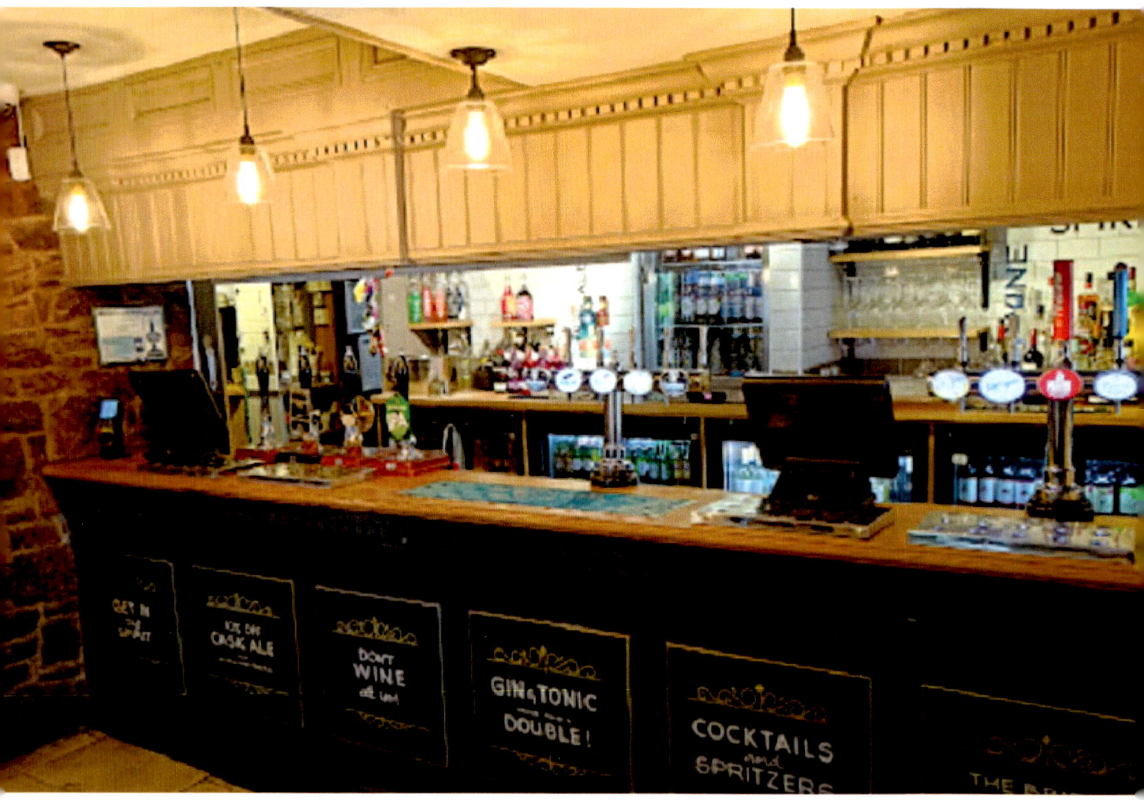

The main bar area at the Shrew.

The small outside area provides an excellent opportunity to sit and watch the proceedings.

Fine food and real ale are available throughout the year and it can get very busy in the evening and at weekends, but as the pub is not large it creates a good atmosphere and is such a good example of an old-fashioned village pub that it should be cherished. At quieter times as you sit there with a pint or glass of wine, it is difficult to imagine that The Shrew is part of a bustling town – it can feel a world apart.

11. The Refreshment Rooms, Rock Ferry

It is hard now to visualise what the area around The Refreshment Rooms once looked like as it is now projects a rather forlorn and careworn outlook. In the early years of the nineteenth century, however, the area was one of the busiest ferry terminals on the Wirral side of the Mersey, boasting not only a fine group of ferry buildings but also the imposing Royal Rock Hotel, which stood in its own grounds, grandly named The Olympian Gardens, which was utilised for entertainments by visiting poirrots and other distractions. The nearby esplanade included cottages that provided hot and cold baths for residents and visitors for a small fee. The close proximity of the magnificent Victorian estate of villas called Rock Park completed the ensemble. All bar the pub and a small part of Rock Park has been swept away over time.

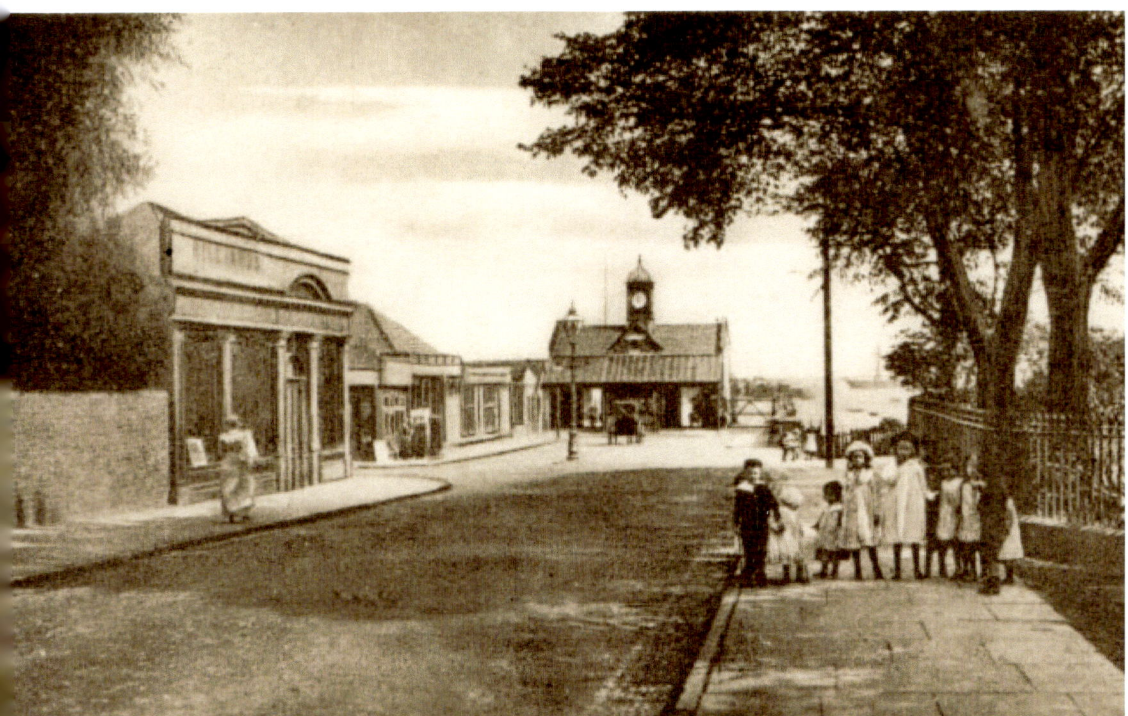

The Refreshment Rooms pictured on a postcard from 1905.

The Refreshment Rooms, however, provide a little oasis in all this devastation and the views across the Mersey remain. The pub was erected around the same time as the Royal Rock Hotel and began its days as The Rock but this was quickly changed to The Refreshment Rooms and traded under this name until 1959 other than a brief spell in the 1880s as The Royal Navy Hotel, probably a nod to the navy training ships moored offshore. As with all the pubs next to the ferry terminals on the Wirral side, the Refreshment Rooms provided food and drink to the thousands of travellers who regularly used the ferries to get to their places of work over in Liverpool. With the closure of the ferry in June 1939, however, the pub struggled to survive and it is a minor miracle that it was not torn down with the other ferry buildings and the hotel, especially as it was further isolated when the Rock Ferry Bypass ripped through Bedford Road, cutting the pub off from the station and the rest of the town.

Having changed its name to The Admiral in 1959, the pub soldiered on until 2007 when it finally closed. After five years, however, it was refurbished by a consortium of members of the neighbouring Royal Mersey Yacht Club and reopened as The Refreshment Rooms again. And what a great job they made of it; no plastic beams and ghastly décor here, and many of the original features have been retained along with some exciting additions, principally the installation of a fine chandelier from The Cunard Building, light fittings from the Adelphi and Lewis's and a solid mahogany bar top which started life rather oddly in the science block of Wirral

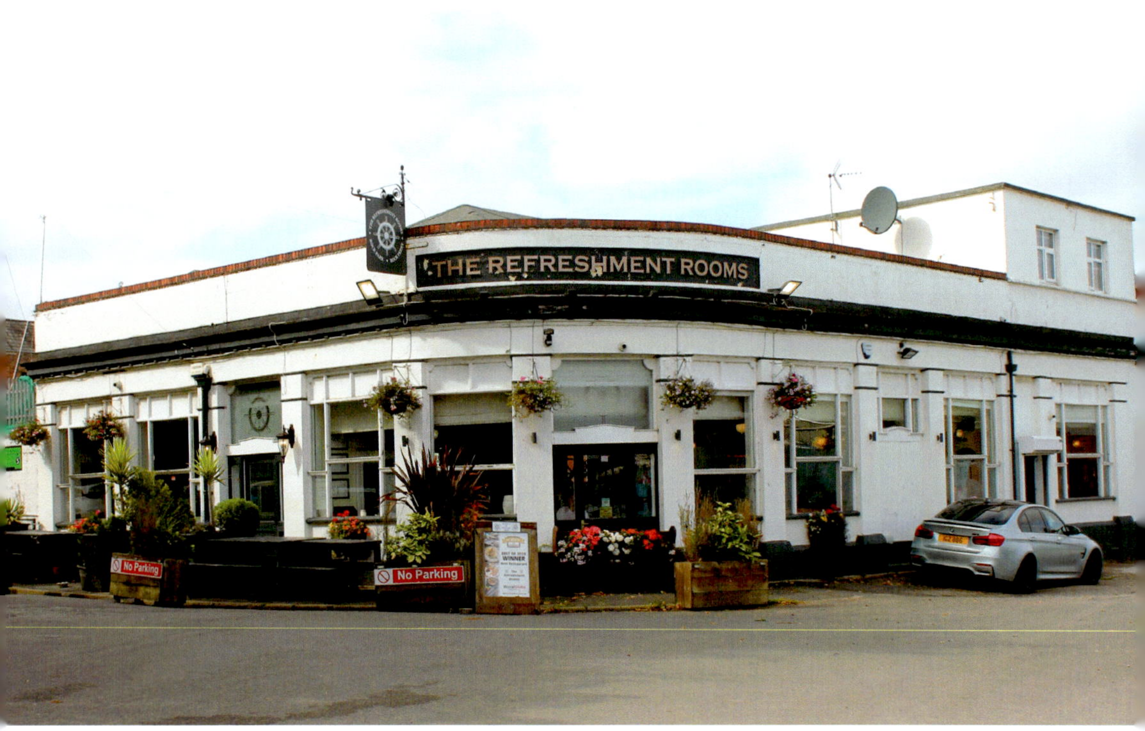

The Refreshment Rooms in 2024.

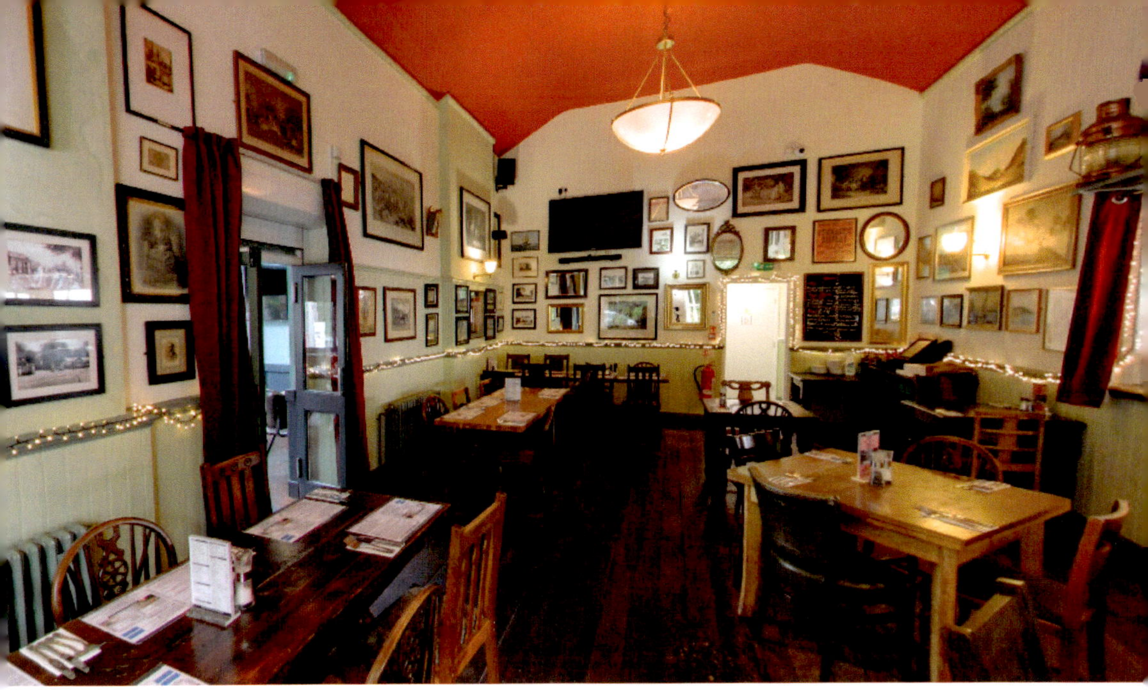

The large dining area in The Refreshment Rooms.

Grammar School. It is a lesson in how to revamp a tired pub and has deservedly gone from strength to strength, building up a reputation for fine food. So much so that it is difficult to visit only for a drink nowadays. It is well worth the adventure of getting there though.

12. The White Lion, West Kirby

Although positioned on the main road from West Kirby to Chester, The White Lion is easy to miss, especially if one is travelling down into the town from the Heswall direction. As is the case with Gallaghers in Birkenhead, the White Lion has a small, narrow front but also goes back through a narrow bar and into a very long but narrow beer garden, replete with its own fish pond and very large goldfish. A new sports marquee is a welcome addition for footy fans. This area forms a wonderful sun trap in the summer.

The pub itself is very traditional with stone floors and proper wooden beams, and is full of interesting nooks and crannies. It is also rather dark and it is easy to imagine it in the Victorian era, enveloped in smoke, full of yokels smoking their long clay pipes whilst caressing a pint of Fuddles Old Dirigible. This rather Troglodyte experience was, of course, a men-only affair. This whole ethos was briefly turned on its head, however, in 1974 when Margaret Richardson took over the pub. After experiencing an unpleasant visit to a male-dominated pub where she was subjected to misogynistic abuse, she decided that part of the White Lion would become a ladies-only bar. As rather sneeringly reported in the *Associated Press* at the time, 'The click of knitting needles has replaced the thunk of darts, and martinis perched on tables once splattered with the foam of ale. Not surprisingly

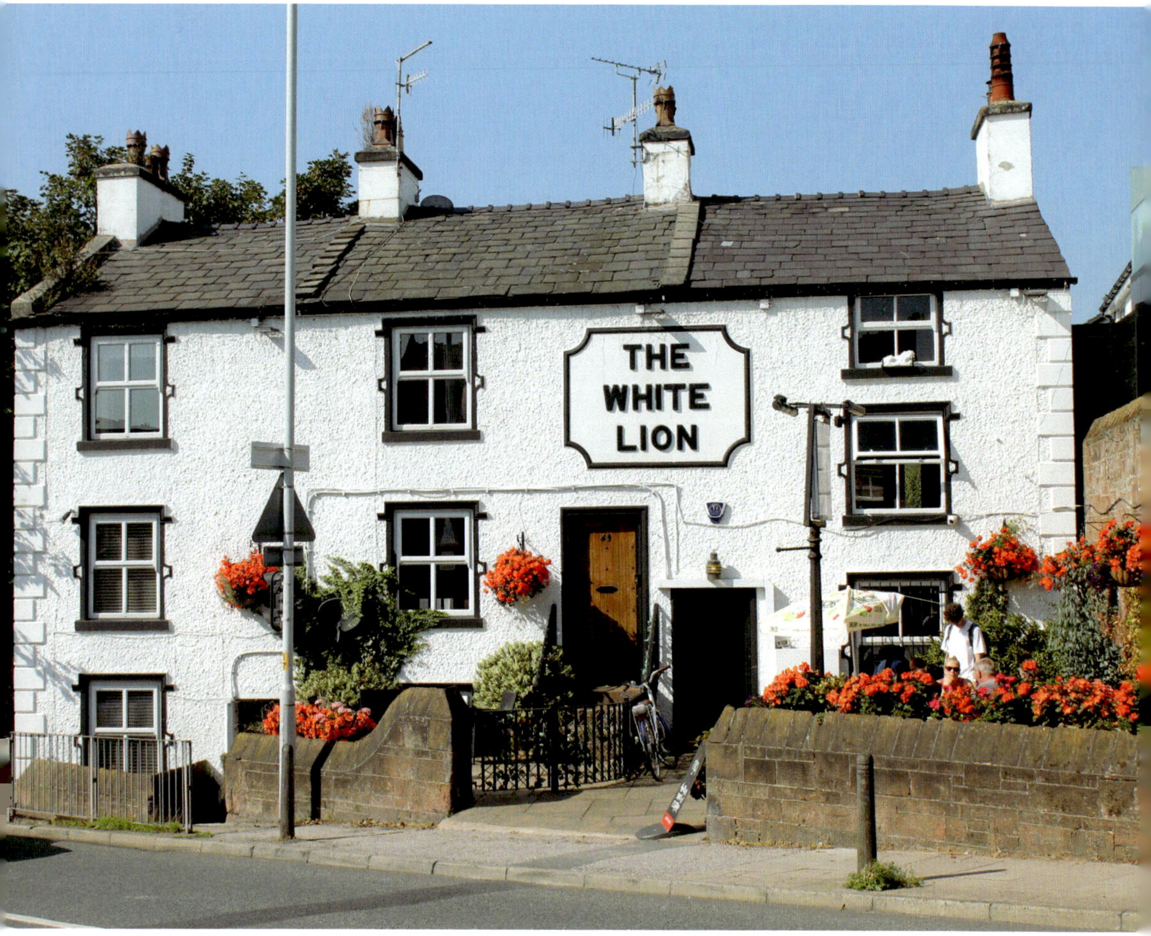

The White Lion in West Kirby, 2024.

the White Lions owner is a woman, but Margaret Richardson doesn't claim to be a Womens Libber. She wanted to open a place where women could go for a drink without being humiliated, ogled, or assumed to be an easy pickup. The Ladies Only bar ... doesn't make money'. This was still the time of Andy Capp, Bernard Manning and *Life on Mars*, and would probably fall foul of today's sex discrimination laws.

Having been briefly called The Lion Inn around 1890, the White Lion was taken over in 1904 by the Birkenhead Brewery at a cost of £3,200. The sale included two attached cottages to sweeten the deal. The pub was run by members of the Ryan family from 1950 until 1974, originally by Tommy Ryan and latterly by his son, both of whom had been licensees in Birkenhead pubs, Tommy at the Canada Hotel before it was bombed out and his son Frank at the Bank of Ireland before his daughter Nancy took over the license. Birkenhead Brewery ran it without event for fifty years until they had a corporate breakdown and unforgivably proposed

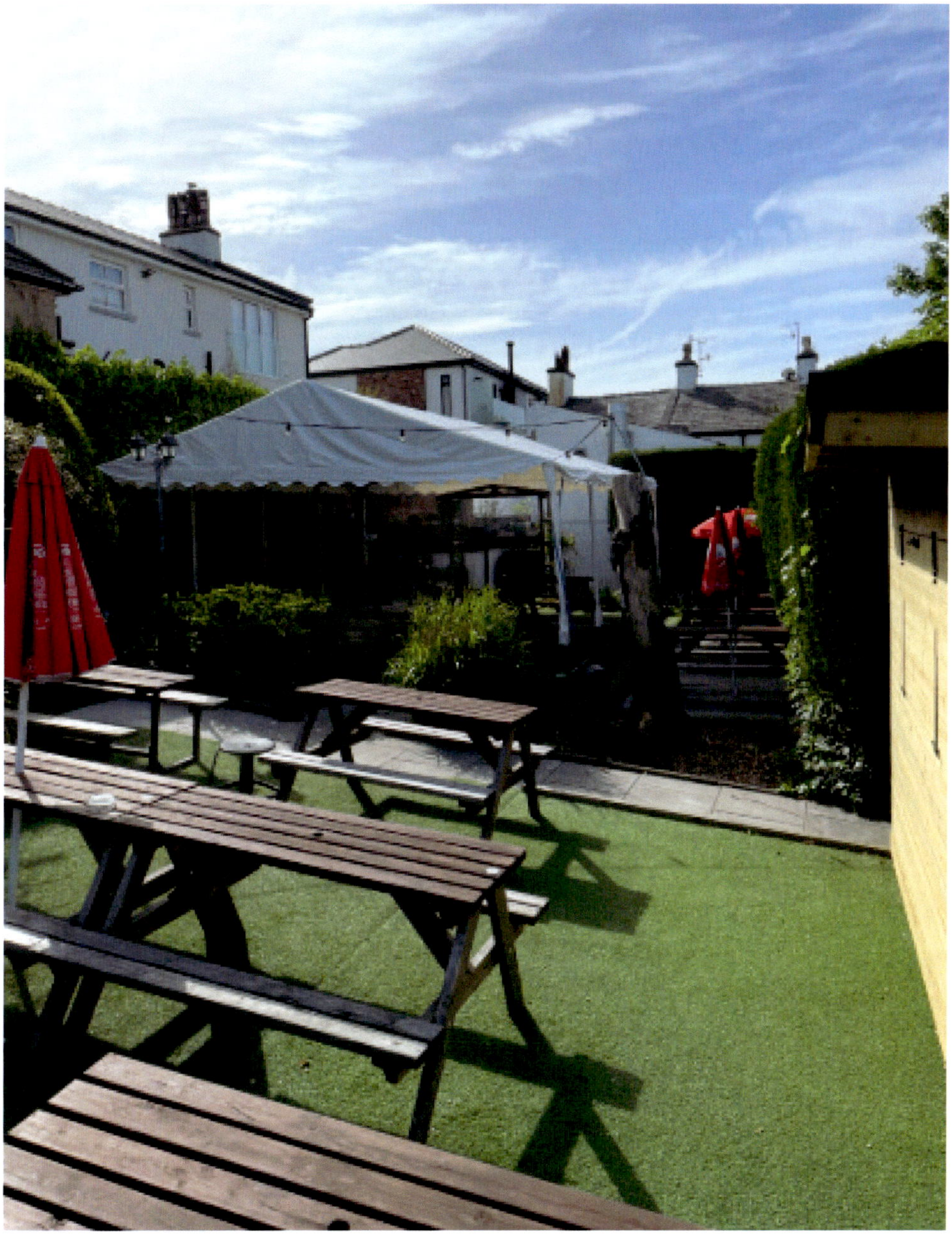

The beer/sports garden behind the White Lion in West Kirby.

demolishing the old pub and rebuilding it, no doubt in the hideous fashion of the time. Luckily common sense for once prevailed and the pub remains its original, delightful self.

Try spotting the little white lion in the small outside drinking area in front of the pub as you while away the time on a hot summer's day.

13. The Ring O' Bells, West Kirby

Having started life as a small farmer's cottage, possibly on the site of an earlier inn, the proud owners of the newly built property broadcast their ownership with a datestone marked 'I r Male 1810 for Isaac and Rebekah Male'. As it was a prime spot in the older part of West Kirby, a beer licence was soon applied for and in 1824 the cottage became a pub, named the Ring of Bells as with many pubs that were within earshot of the local church. The beer licence stated sternly that the premises 'shall not suffer any gambling with cards, draughts, dice, bagatelle ... nor permit or suffer any bull, bear or badger baiting, cock fighting or other such sport or amusement'. Quite where they would find space to bait a bull, or a bear for that matter, is not noted. Faced with such Draconian restrictions the landlord settled eventually for bowls, a bowling green being created to the back of the property in 1897 with a fine pavilion. It also boasted a tennis court at one time.

The cellars for the pub were carved out of the sandstone bedrock below and extended underneath Village Road, the rock having been shaped to hold the barrels of ale, with a drainage channel below. In the early days it was claimed that the romantic poets Shelley and Keats and the artist J. M. W. Turner were regular visitors. It is a

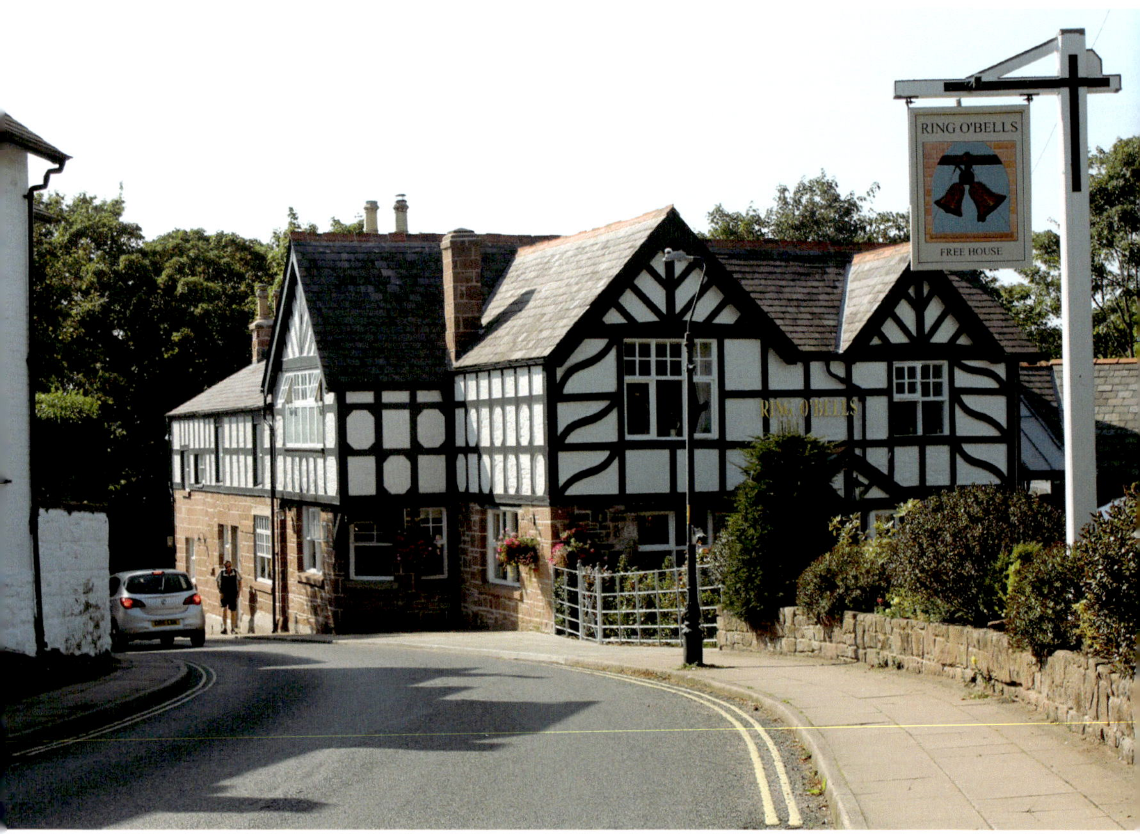

The Ring O' Bells in 2024.

spurious claim that the poets popped in for a quick half but it is possible that Turner drank in the bar after a hard day's daub as he is known to have favoured the light at West Kirby for some of his fiery sunsets. Malcolm Lowry, the poet and author, not the more famous painter, lived in nearby Caldy, and mentioned the Ring O' Bells in his writing.

A contemporary advertisement gives a good idea of the pub at the time: 'Good accommodation and Liberal Table Dinners and picnics catered for, Open and Closed carriages for hire'. The author of this puff was the proprietor, the wonderfully named W. H. Poingdestre. Change finally came in a big way in 1994 when the centuries old fug of tobacco and spilt ale gave way to the aromas of bloater cutlets and pufferfish *en croûte* in a stickleback jus, as the pub became an exclusive fish restaurant in 1994. Not proving a hit with the locals, however, it reverted to a pub a few years later and would have no doubt carried on as before but for the pandemic, which, as with all hospitality outlets, hit the pub hard. It closed for refurbishment and has recently reopened with several large extensions and dining areas. Time will tell if this is a

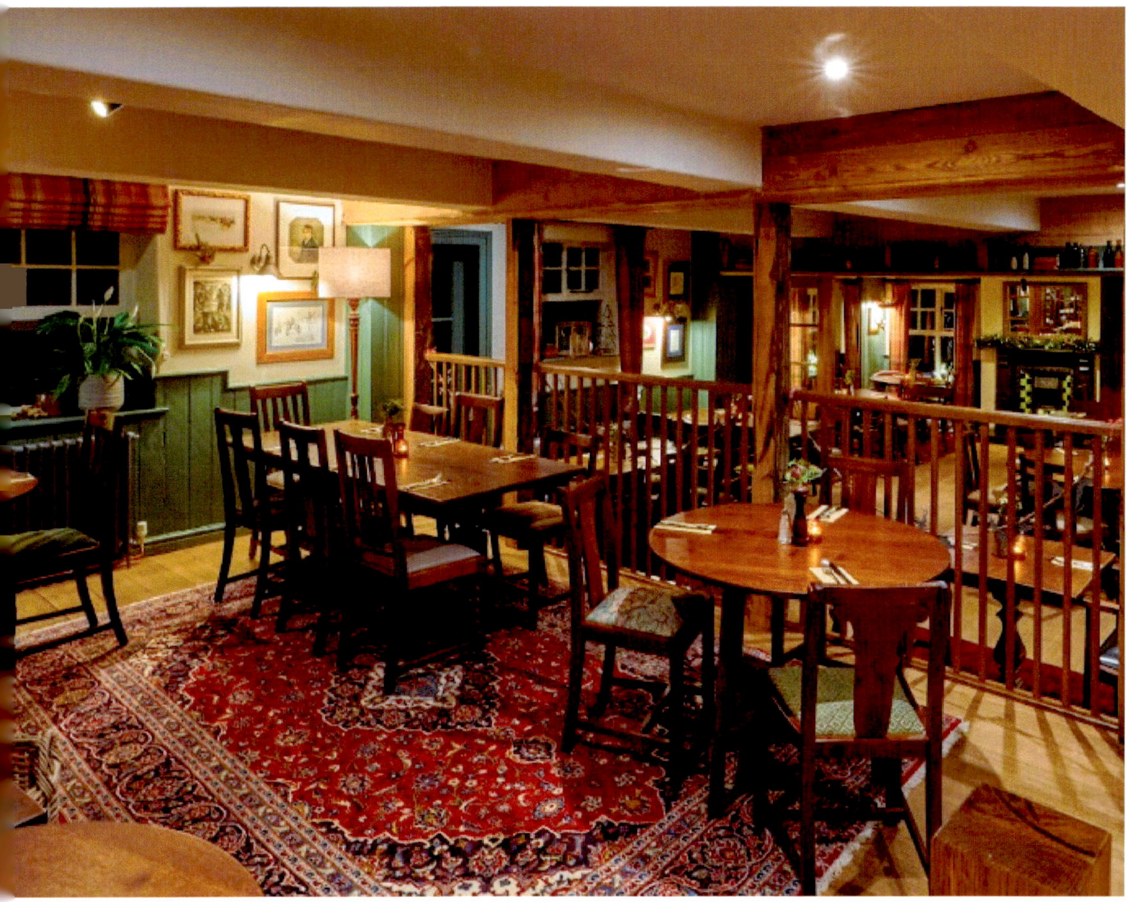

Part of the new dining area in The Ring O' Bells.

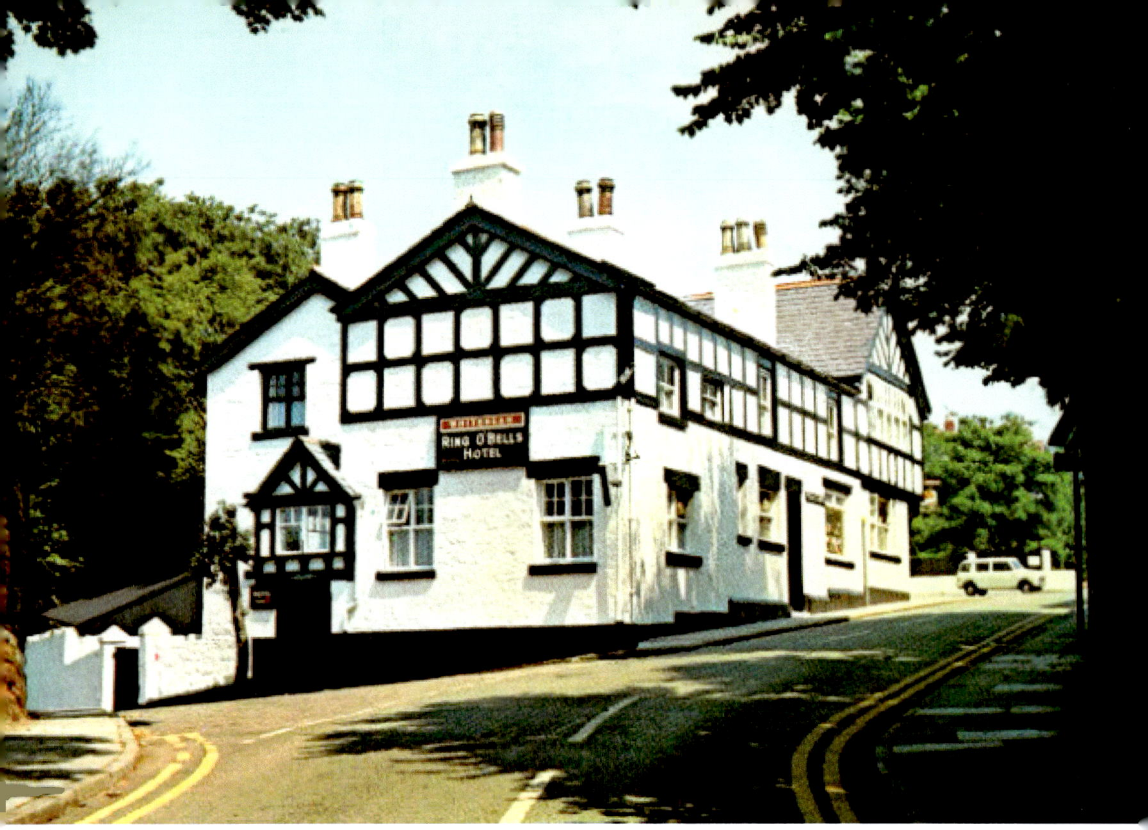

1960s postcard showing The Ring O'Bells.

success. Before closing for the refit the pub had a final hurrah when a Freddie Mercury tribute act entertained the locals. A fine night was had by all, especially when, during his rendition of 'I Want to Break Free' one of the staff started following him around with a vacuum cleaner in homage to the famous video for the song. Times like these are what make a great pub.

14. The Dee Hotel, West Kirby

Kirby is an old Norse name meaning 'church town', with West Kirby being one of many villages in this part of Wirral ending in 'By', indicating that there was much Viking settlement in these parts. 'West' was added to the name to differentiate it from 'Kirbea in Walea', or Wallasey. Archaeological finds in the area including stone tools and coins prove that the area was inhabited far earlier than this, however.

Before the coming of the railways West Kirby was a sleepy backwater with the more populous part being centred in what is now termed the Lower Village where the Ring of Bells lies. The land now occupied by The Dee Hotel was originally the site of a group of houses called Dee Bank, with a pair of cottages known as Yew Tree House and Yew Tree Cottage directly opposite. The cottages were demolished to make way for the Wirral Lines railway station when it was extended through from Liverpool, the houses opposite being torn down to make way for The Dee

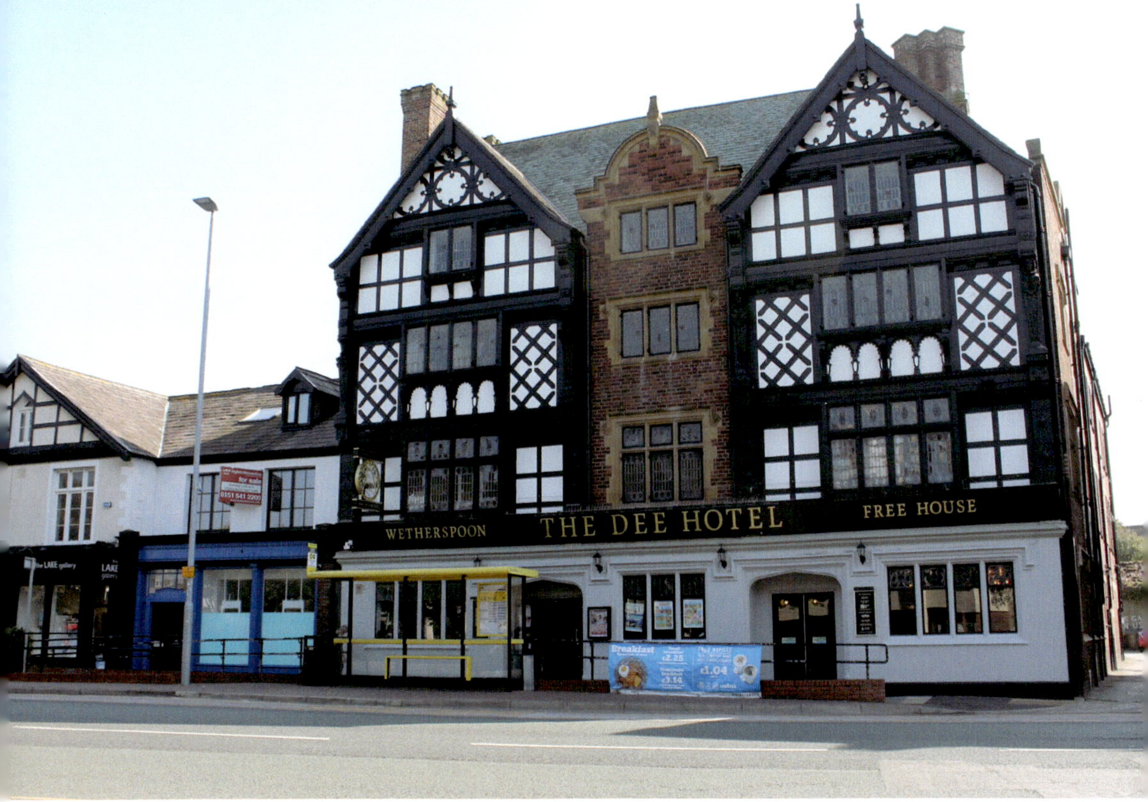

Wetherspoons Dee Hotel in 2024.

Hotel soon afterwards. As with the pubs near to the ferry termini, the hotel was built to provide refreshments and boarding for travellers, and received a massive boost when the Hooton railway line was extended through to Caldy and West Kirby in 1886.

The hotel proved immensely popular and was later extended into the adjacent stationery shop when Walkers of Warrington took over the premises in the 1930s. After the Second World War, however, passenger numbers fell and the West Kirby to Hooton Railway closed in 1956, becoming The Wirral Way Linear Park in 1973. It was eventually taken over by J D Wetherspoon in 2001 and has become one of the most popular 'Spoons on Wirral, despite being threatened with closure several times. As with most Wetherspoon pubs, efforts have been made to retain and enhance the original features with much old panelling and stained glass in evidence, the exterior being left in its mock-Tudor livery. There was talk of making it into a hotel again but the air conditioning installed in the former bedrooms would have made the cost prohibitive.

Wetherspoon pubs are not to everyone's liking, with some of the opinions voiced in the national press being deplorably snobbish and ill-informed, but it cannot be denied that they have rescued and restored many fine old buildings which would otherwise have been destroyed or converted beyond recognition, and have raised over £20 million for Clic Sargent Childrens Charity. They also provide an outlet for many local brewers, which surely must be a good thing. Their involvement in CAMRA and Casque Marque has helped to promote real ale throughout the country and regular beer tasting events have been held at The Dee, coupled with their quarterly beer festivals showcasing many local ales.

15. The Green Lodge, Hoylake

Dating back as far as 1750, The Green Lodge has seen the rise of Hoylake from a major safe anchorage for ships waiting to enter the Port of Liverpool to a major town and holiday destination. It now forms part of the Kings Gap Conservation Area, so called for the historic departure of William III's army from the beach here en route to the famous Battle of the Boyne in 1690.

It was originally constructed as a shooting lodge for the lord of the manor, Sir John Stanley, but as the area rose in popularity due to the increase in sea bathing and its assumed health benefits, the Stanleys realised its potential for making money and constructed The Royal Hotel close by the lodge to cater for the influx of soggy patrons. The Royal Hotel has now gone but the Green Lodge was expanded as a newer group of travellers arrived in the area via the new Mersey railway terminus in 1866. The Victorian travellers were here not to fling themselves into the Briney, however, but to pootle about on the vast expanses of sand not two minutes walk from the hotel. The Green Lodge had the added advantage at the time of exclusive rights for its patrons to shoot rabbits on The Warren (now the Royal Liverpool Golf Course).

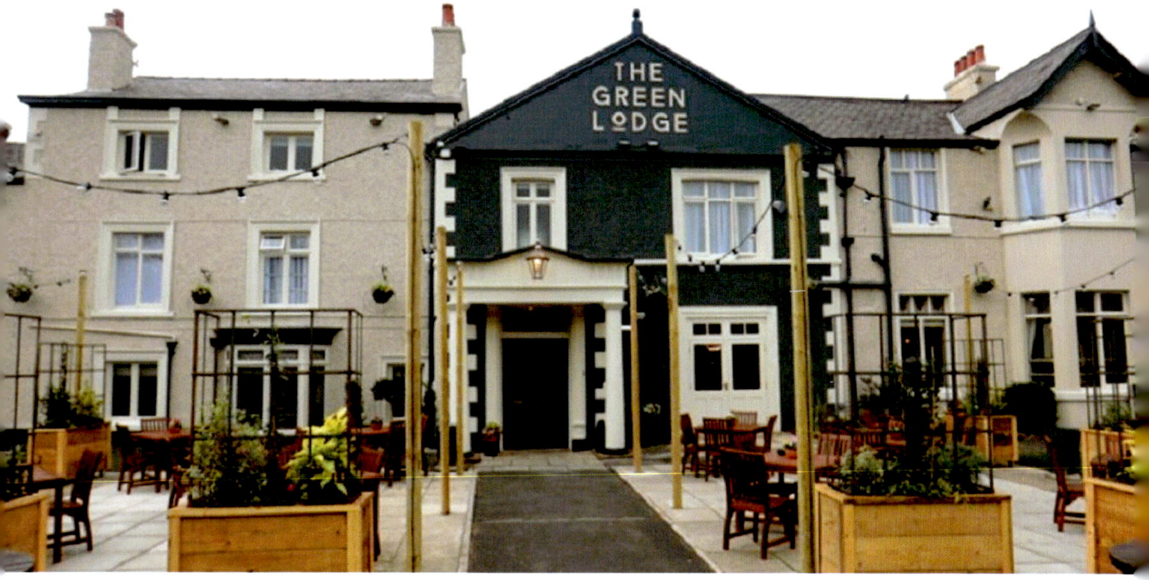

The Green Lodge in 2024.

Even before the advent of the railway, much trade was produced by an omnibus service that went from the Green Lodge through to Goughs Woodside Hotel, which ran, or rather trotted, every morning and evening, for the benefit of businessmen who worked in Liverpool. One other major advantage for the Green Lodge was its proximity to the Royal Liverpool Golf Links, which expanded at this time from a nine-hole course and attendant racecourse to the internationally renowned course it is today.

A contemporary advertising puff for The Green Lodge ran in that very Victorian prose: 'The salubrious climate of Hoylake renders it one of the most healthy seaside and golfing resorts in England'. The latter boast still holds true but the seaside element is being slowly diminished by the growth of sparta grass on the sands, a deliberate plan by the council to encourage wildlife but a policy which divides opinion.

The Lodge was run by Burtonwood Brewery in the 1950s and it was around this time that they had a men-only bar called the Tudor Room, which had pictures of the regulars placed on the walls and their own beer tankards hung about the place, including one for the local vicar whose personal vessel held a quarter of a gallon (i.e. two pints). It is now run by Marston's on a more inclusive basis and has a very large, well-appointed beer garden since its renovation in 2013, which was completed just in time for the British Open Golf Championship.

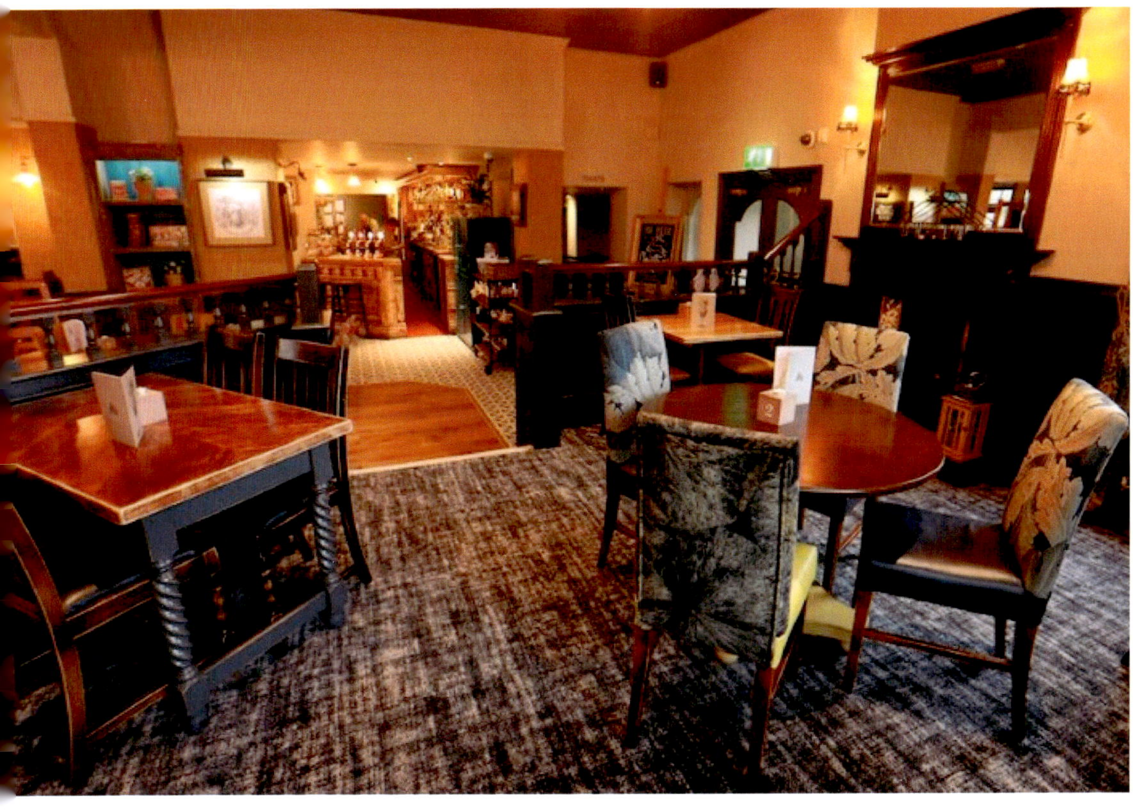

Inside The Green Lodge in 2022.

16. The Railway Inn, Meols

There would appear to be plenty of things buried under car parks in this country, notably the long-lost remains of one of our more notably villainous kings, Richard III, disinterred in 2012 from a car park in Leicester. The good people of Wirral can top that, however; not a mere body but an entire Viking longship if you please, discovered under the car park at the front of The Railway Inn at Meols. The old clinker boat lies a few feet below the surface in waterlogged blue clay and its dimensions have been confirmed by 'geofizz'. The area, originally called Meir meaning 'sandhills', is of Nordic origin so it may come as less of a surprise to find one of their craft buried here.

All this excitement may be rather lost on your average punter, however, who just wants to visit a large friendly pub with plenty of television screens, ideal for watching the football on a Sunday afternoon. And The Railway Inn certainly ticks all these boxes. The original inn was built in 1866 to catch the passing trade at nearby Meols station from passengers using the railway from Liverpool to West Kirby, but the pub we see now was constructed to cater for a different type of passing trade – that of the motor car. With the increase in car ownership in the 1930s brewers were quick to see a business opportunity and built three large and very similar pubs on Wirral. The current Railway Inn was built in 1938 on the main road from Birkenhead to West Kirby, The Arrowe Park was built at the same time on the busy crossroads from Birkenhead to Greasby and Moreton, while the Pensby Hotel (now demolished) lay on the road through to Heswall.

The Railway Inn at Meols, 2024.

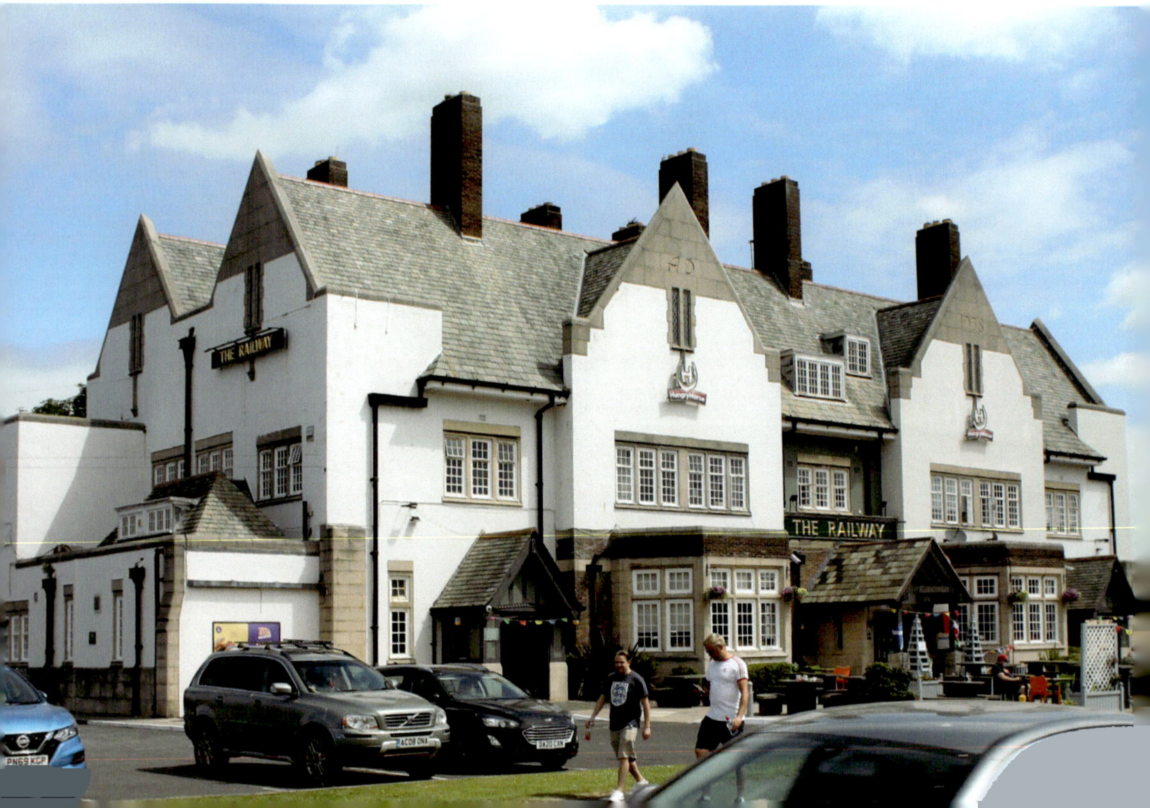

There is more to attract people into the Railway besides footy on the telly. As a Hungry Horse, their food and drink offerings are comprehensive and popular, as is their regular special afternoon offerings of local singers and tribute acts. There is talk of digging up the longboat in the near future, which can only add to its popularity and could gain it national interest. Perhaps the Lagina brothers from 'The Curse of Oak Island' should try digging for the Ark of the Covenant in Meols rather than spending their time in The Money Pit in Canada?

17. The Irby Mill, Greasby

The current advertising puff for the Irby Mill pretty much sums up how the pub appears today: 'a traditional sandstone country pub on the border of Greasby and Irby. Dog friendly'. It could also add that it serves a constantly rotating selection of real ales, serves excellent food and boasts a large outside area. It looks as if the pub has been here since time immemorial but it was only opened as the Irby Mill in 1980. The actual mill was built in the early eighteenth century to replace an even earlier mill which had burnt down, a common problem with mills, especially if their sails are not battened down before high winds appear. A miller's cottage was built beside it in the early 1800s and this was the structure that survived after the mill ceased working in the 1880s and was pulled down in 1898. The cottage continued to make money when it began providing teas and snacks for the many walkers and cyclists hereabouts. The enterprise proved so successful that it was

The old postbox outside the Irby Mill.

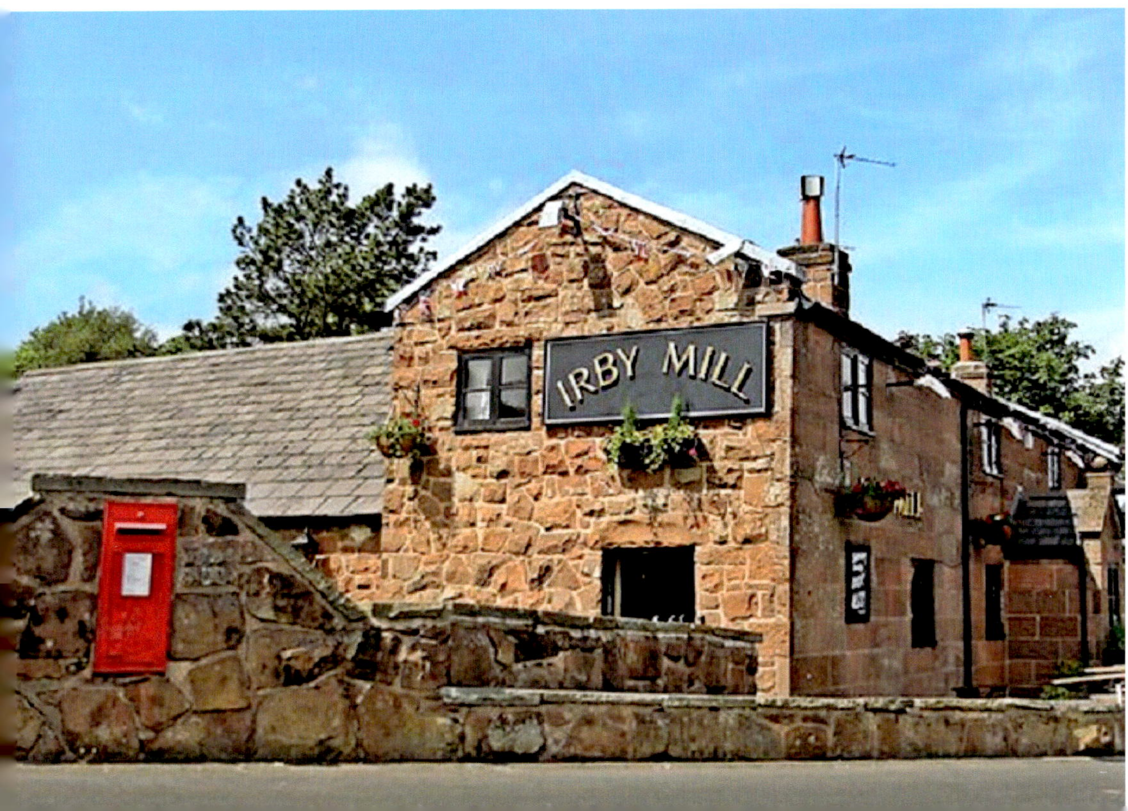

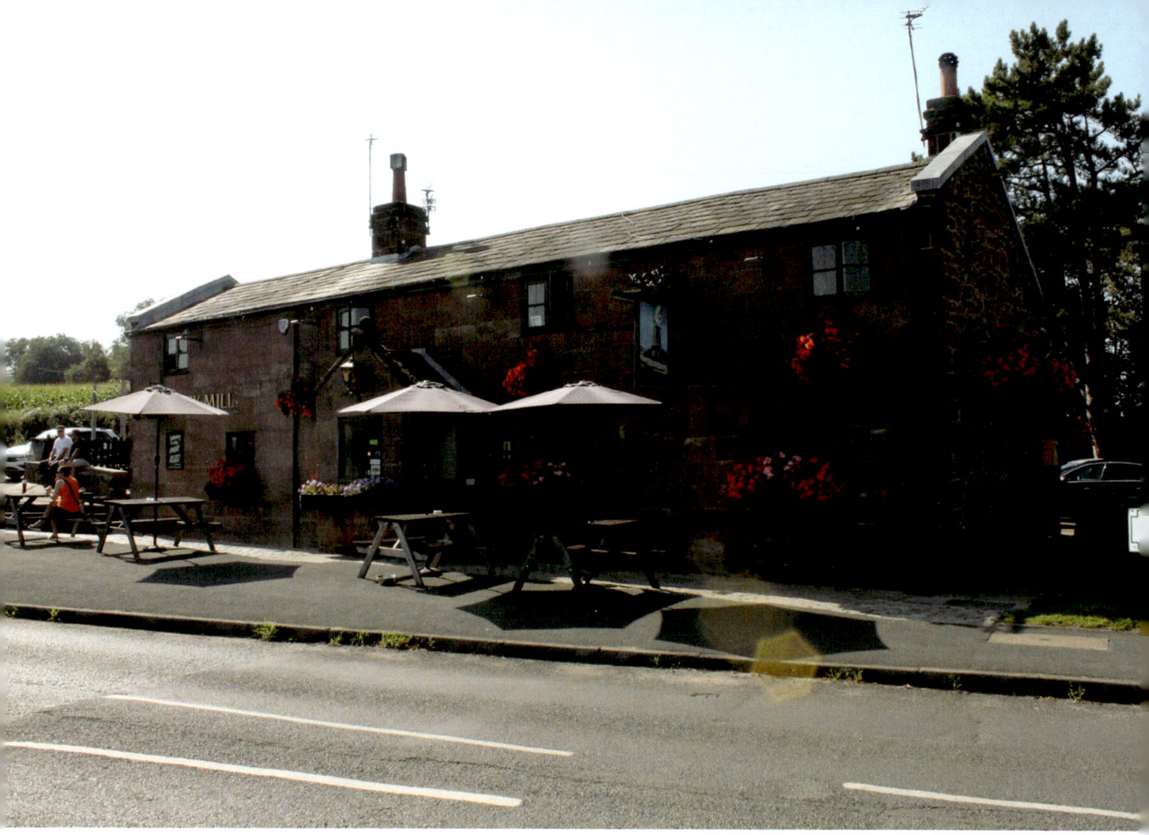

The Irby Mill pub in 2024.

fully converted to a café in 1924 when the owners George and Bertha Lumsden christened it 'The Old Mill Café', a name that was clearly torn from their creative souls.

The business savvy Lumsdens extended the property and opened it as a dance hall in the 1930s, which again proved a smart move, so much so that Higsons saw the potential of the place and bought it off the Lumsdens in 1938, although the building remained as a café right through the 1960s. Higsons attempted to gain planning permission for an extended pub premises but these plans were rejected until 1979 when permission was given to pull down the Lumsden extension and build a new one better suited to its use as a pub. During this period the Merseyside Archaeological Society were allowed to pootle about on the site before the new work was commenced but nothing of national importance was found, although remnants of an even earlier structure were discovered. A two-storey extension was finished in 1980 using matching sandstone blocks, which makes the current building appear all of one period and a fine job they made of it too.

The pub still provides a welcome haven for walkers and cyclists along with motorists and a warm welcome is always guaranteed. Things to look out for include a rare Edward VII postbox on the wall outside and a fireplace confusingly dated 1780–1980 – these dates actually refer to the anniversary of Higsons Brewery rather than anything to do with the Irby Mill pub or its history.

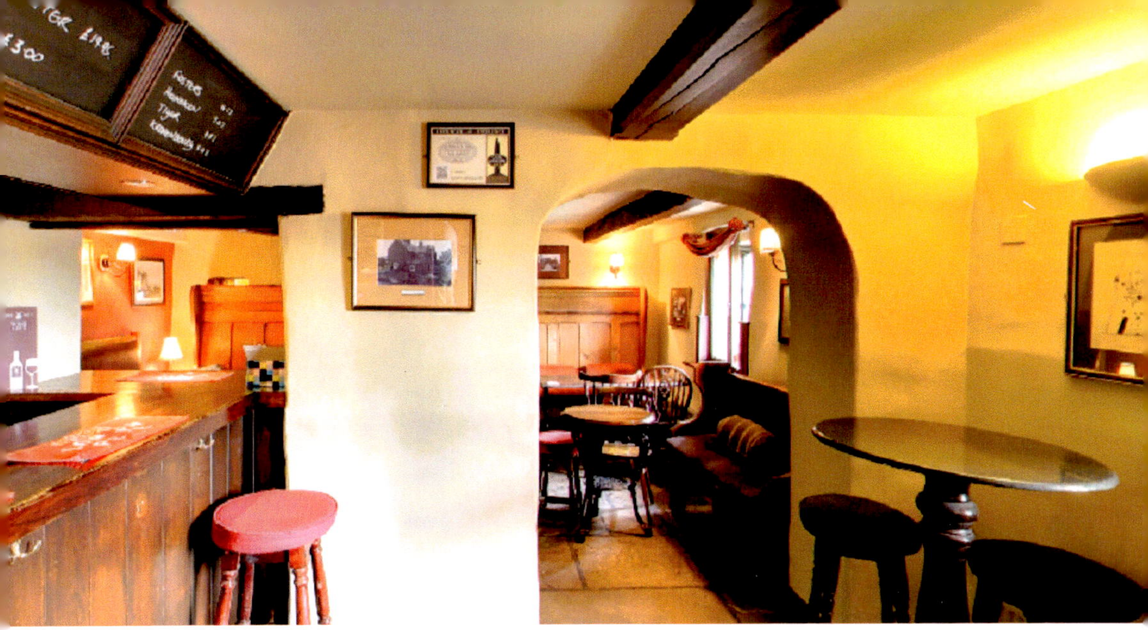

A quiet moment in the busy Irby Mill.

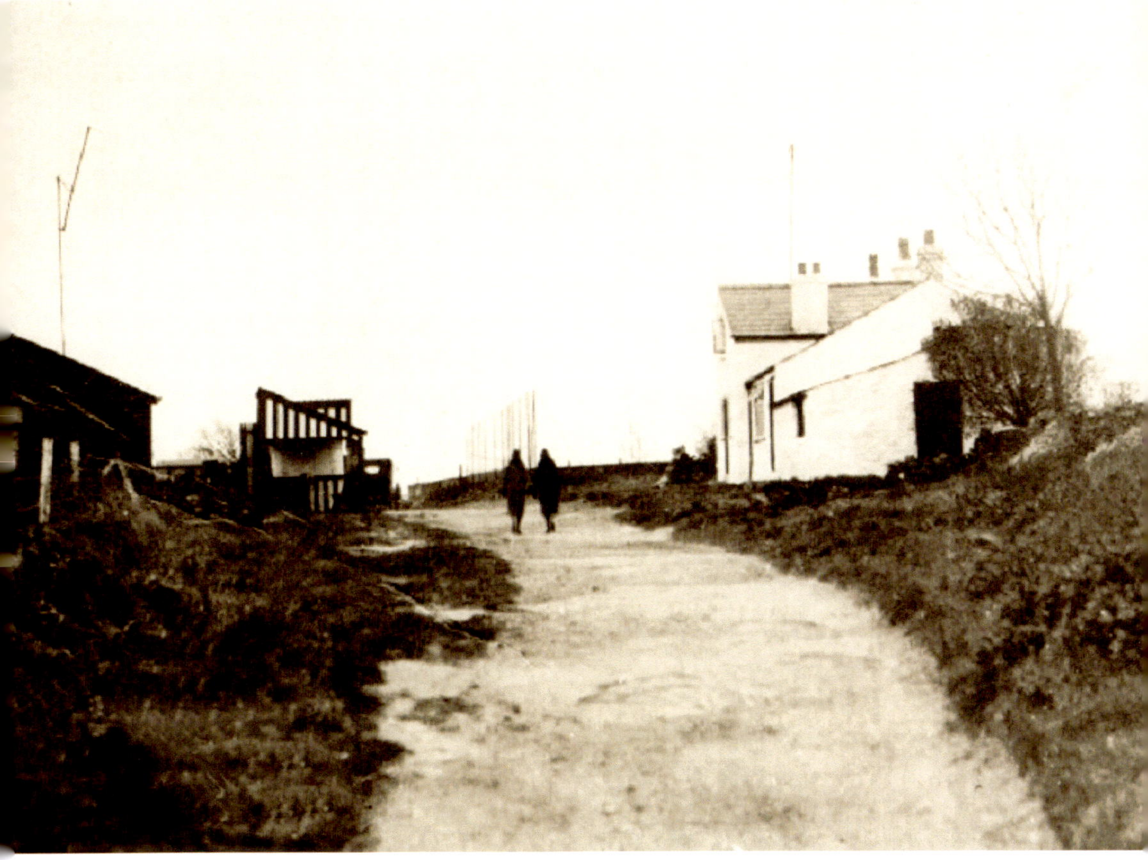

The Irby Mill before conversion to a pub.

18. The Fox and Hounds, Barnston

The Fox and Hounds is a contender for the most renamed pub in Wirral. This is most unusual for a country pub as it is usually the urban pubs that have their names changed from The Rose and Crown or The Kings Arms to something trendy like the Walnut and Pigs Bladder, Gozzies Place or something similarly ghastly. No historic references, no sense of place, not anything worthwhile really. The Fox, as everyone shortens it to, has, over the years, been known as The Flag, The Hen and Chickens, The Black Horse and The Sportsmans Arms.

The site has been the location for licensed premises for nearly 400 years. Its first recorded mention is from a tithe map from 1754, which gave one John Harrison as the licensee. In 1822 John Youds was licensee when the pub was known as The Flag and the Youds were still running it as The Hen and Chickens and The Black Horse into the 1830s. The Gertrey family had taken over by the 1890s when another name change to The Sportsmans was recorded. They were to run it for over seventy years. An advertisement of the time related that it had 'one bed for travellers, accommodation and refreshment for ten and stables for two. A modest house, fair accommodation, refreshments other than drink frequently supplied'. Not a particularly ringing endorsement it must be said but more honest than most of today's hyperbolic advertising.

The Fox and Hounds in 2024.

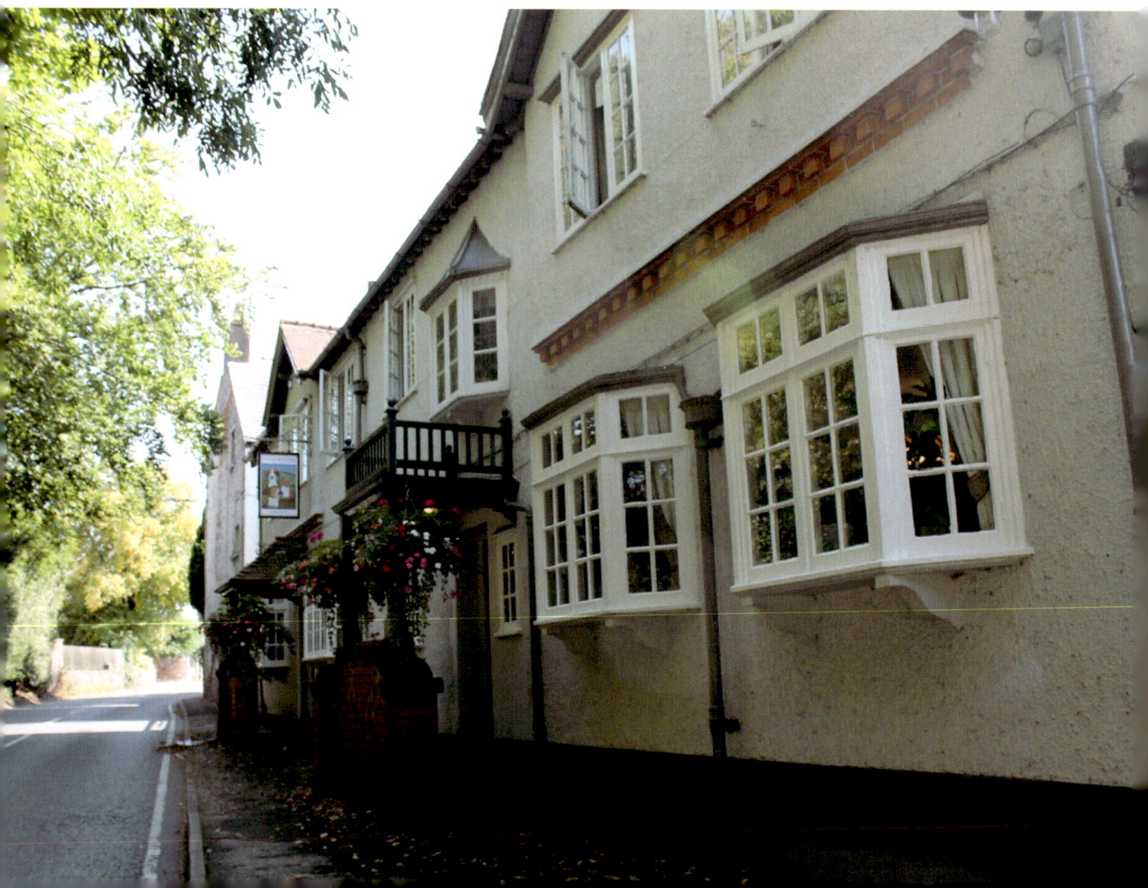

In earlier times pubs would be located in strategically important locations, not just to maximise patronage from passing trade, but also to assist with the day-to-day running of the local community. The local plough was often located next to the pub for example. The Fox and Hounds was probably sited halfway down Barnston Dale, or Barnston Dip as most Wirralians know it, to be able to supply an extra horse to assist with heavy loads being transported up to the top of The Dip. The road outside was notoriously uneven and it would have taken a concerted effort to get loads to where they needed to be. The road has, of course, been widened and metalled since then but care still needs to be taken, especially as customers turn into the car park halfway up the hill.

The Sportsman came down in 1911 when the present building was erected 12 feet back from the site of the demolished pub at a cost of £2,237. It was standard practice to retain the old premises while the new pub was built and then transfer the licence overnight, but as The Sportsman needed to be knocked down before the new build could commence, Birkenhead Brewery had to surrender the licence to The Bull and Dog in Neston and transfer it to The Fox and Hounds when it opened.

The bar at the Fox and Hounds.

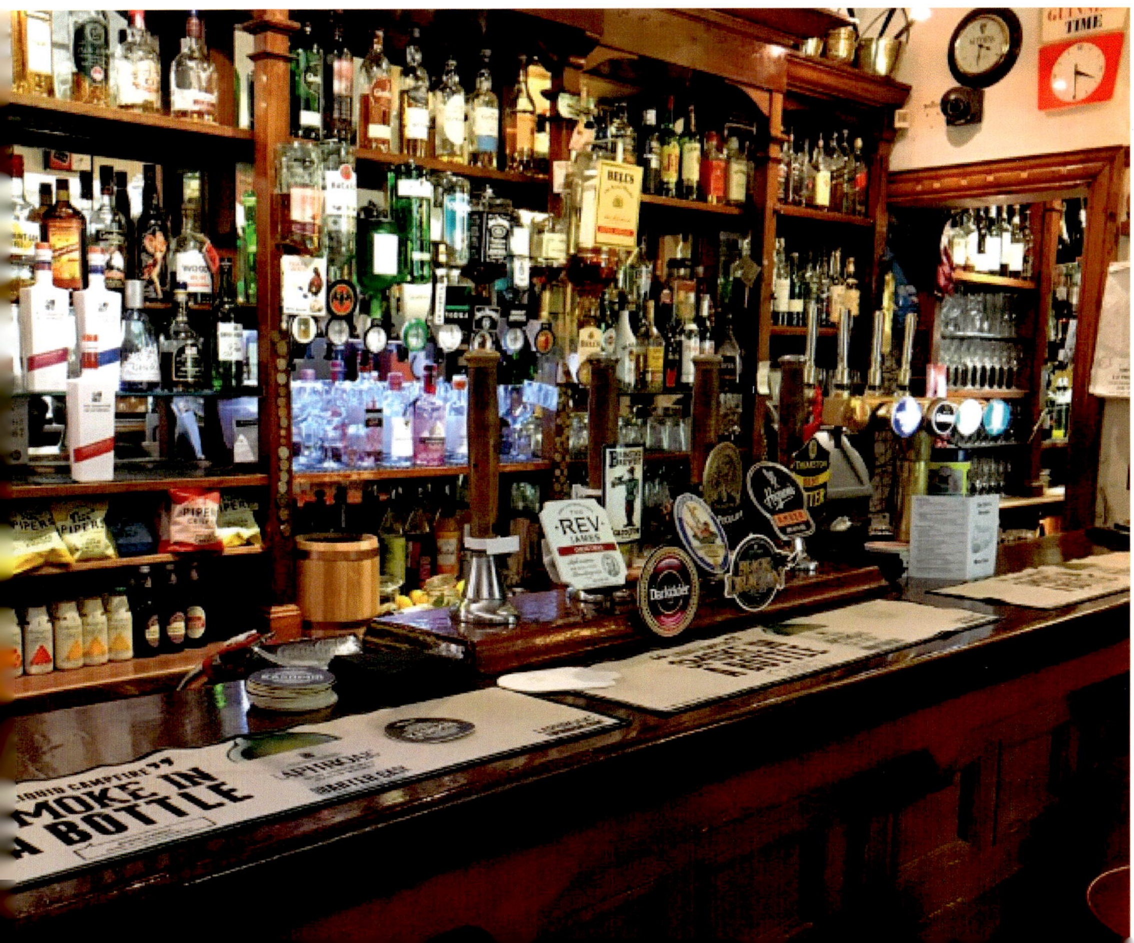

Although built during the reign of George V, the pub contains an abundance of Edwardian detail, including screens with leaded windows and Art Nouveau patterning, plenty of beautifully crafted pine woodwork, and an original bar counter top, a very rare survival, not surprising really considering the hammering it has had over the years by thousands of thirsty yokels. Even the original bell pushes survive in working order, although the landlord keeps them turned off due to over-enthusiastic usage.

Gone are the days when the best a customer could hope for in the way of food was a bag of pork scratchings or an amorphous globule in a pickle jar that would not have looked out of place in a lab. Today, especially after a major refurb, The Fox and Hounds now provides fine dining and fine wines in luxuriant surroundings for the well-heeled punter – what the smock-wearing ploughmen of yesteryear would have made of it all is anyone's guess. A taste of the original ambience, however, is still obtainable with the separate bar at the back, which is satisfyingly boisterous and retains the atmosphere of a traditional country pub.

19. The Glegg Arms, Gayton

The Glegg Arms stands at an important road junction joining the Top Chester Road (A540) with the roads to Barnston and Thornton Hough, and as such has been able to capture much of the passing trade since 1840 when it began life as the unfortunately named Crabbes Inn, named after the original proprietor, one Edward Crabbe Esquire. It changed to The Glegg Arms around 1850 but got the Crabbes again from 1872 until 1881 when it finally settled with the name it retains to this day.

The Gleggs were an ancient and distinguished local family who can trace their ancestry back to the time of the Norman invasion of 1066. The first significant date regarding the Gleggs in the area of the pub was when Gayton passed by marriage to the family in 1330. Further highlights were when Edward Glegg of Calday Grange purchased the Manor of Irby in 1655 and William Glegg founded Calday Grange Grammar School in 1636. Alex Glegg was an ancestor of one of many family members who emigrated from Wirral to the New World and became a member of the Canadian Cricket Team in 1996–97.

That so much history can be tied into the name of a pub speaks volumes for the importance of local hostelries throughout the country and a compelling reason not to change the name into something fanciful and irrelevant on a mere whim. As with most country pubs, the Glegg Arms has been expanded over the years. Up until 1980 expansion was piecemeal, with a public weighbridge being added in the late 1890s and a bowling green in 1904. The weighbridge may seem a strange addition but was popular at the time as an added source of income for the publican. Bowling greens were also very popular, with most country pubs having one tucked round the back and local bowling leagues being set up throughout Wirral.

Major expansion came in 1980 when a Beefeater Steakhouse opened in the pub, with a comprehensive refit to cater for its new role. The Travelodge arrived in 2005 with an enormous expansion at the rear of the pub. It now caters for a completely

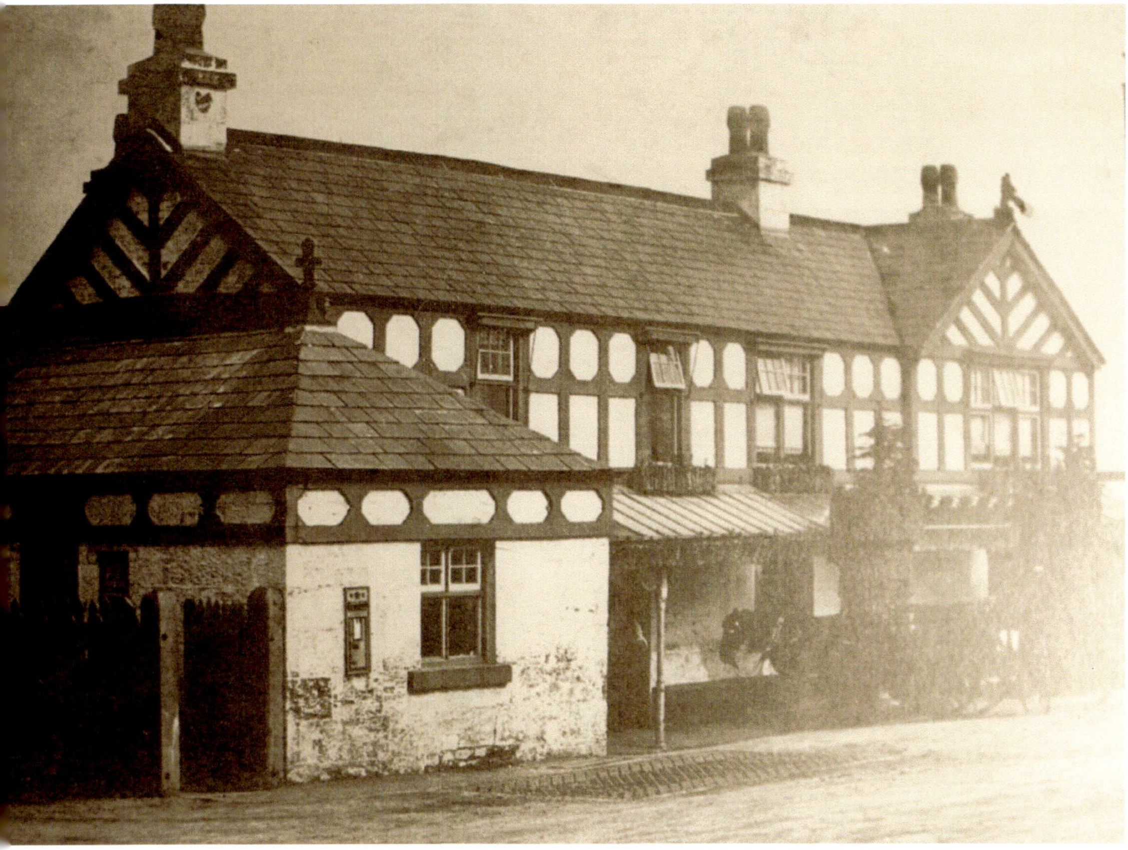

Above: The Glegg Arms on an old postcard of 1908.

Below: The Glegg Arms in 2024.

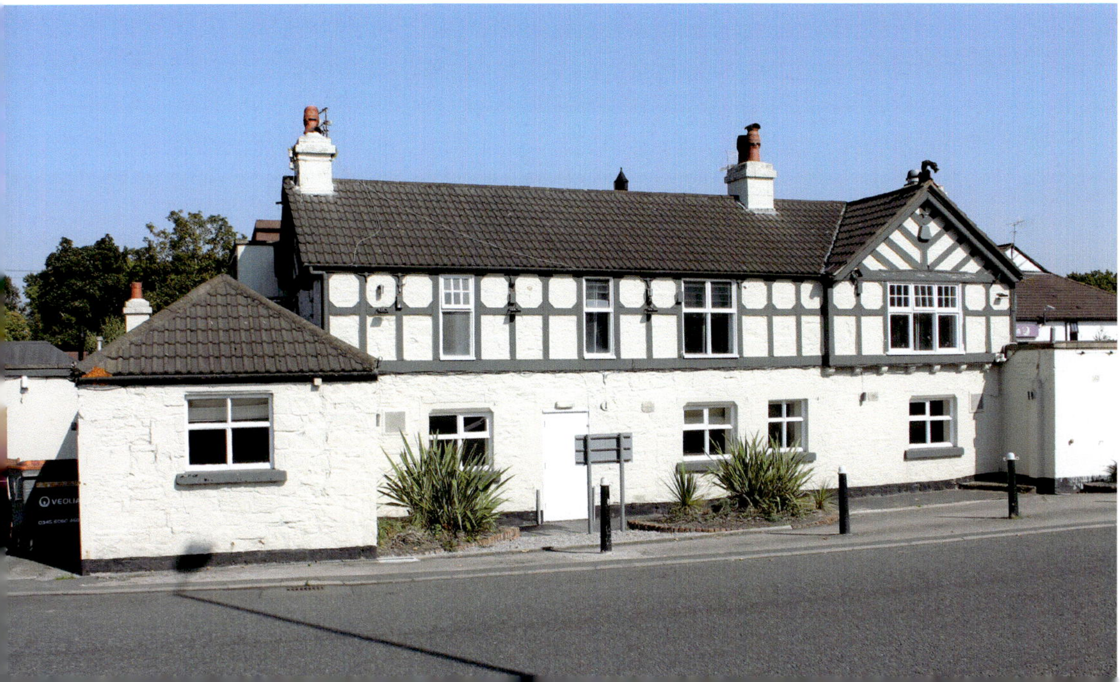

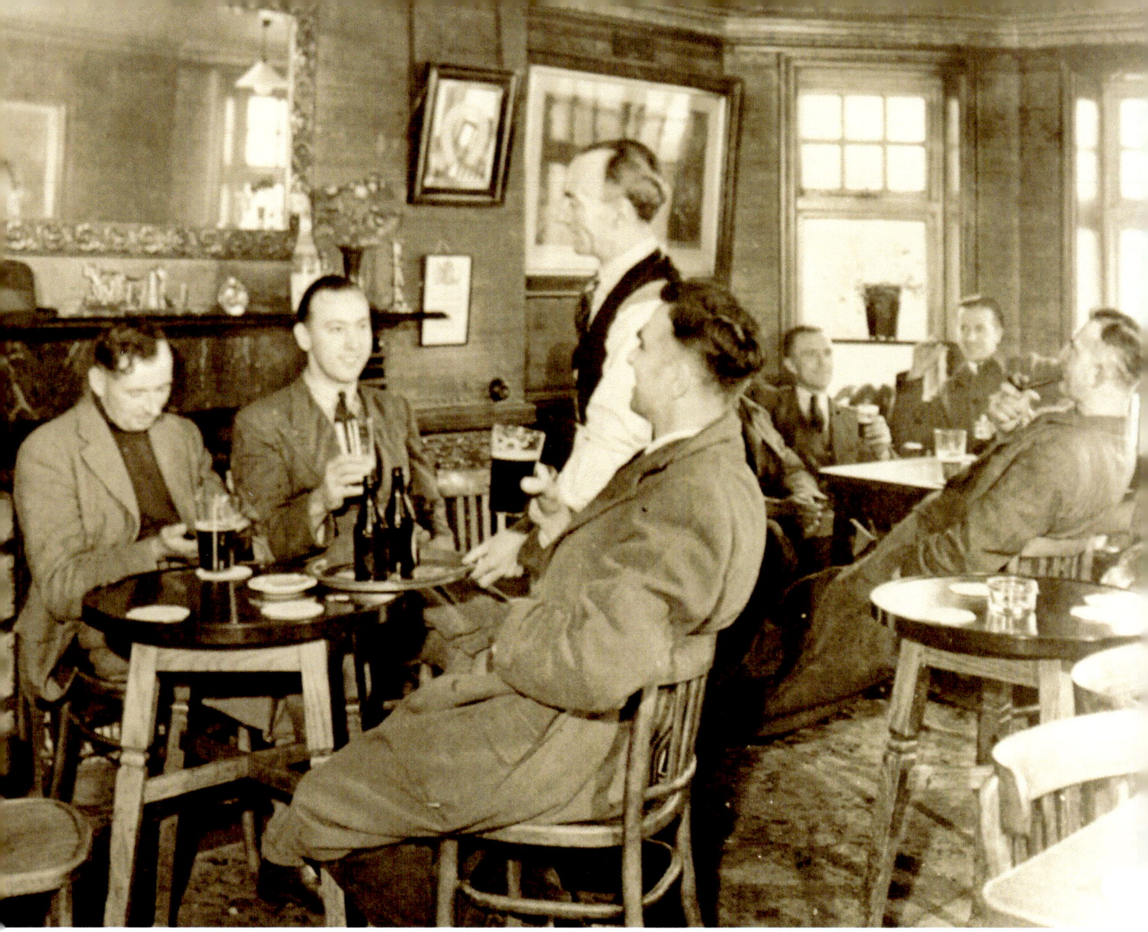

Locals in The Glegg Arms, *c.* 1950.

different clientele from when it was patronised by the local farming community but like most pubs it has had to move with the times and remains a pleasant place to visit for some afternoon refreshment.

20. The Red Lion, Parkgate

It is difficult to imagine nowadays what an important port Parkgate was in the eighteenth and nineteenth centuries when the waters of the Dee still lapped against the sea wall and fishermen sat about mending their nets in the summer heat. The long front still attracts a great many visitors who come for the view or to watch the flocks of birds out in the estuary while they sit and eat the obligatory ice cream or munch on the ever-popular Parkgate shrimps, but back then it catered for travellers to Ireland by boat and Chester by stagecoach. During these heady days Parkgate had no fewer than eighteen inns. The Red Lion is now the oldest of the surviving inns to have remained relatively unchanged. First recorded in 1822, it was run by members of the Wood family for most of the nineteenth century. Lee Wood held the licence in the 1850s and 1860s and was appropriately also a joiner. Like most local publicans of the time, he needed some other trade to supplement his income.

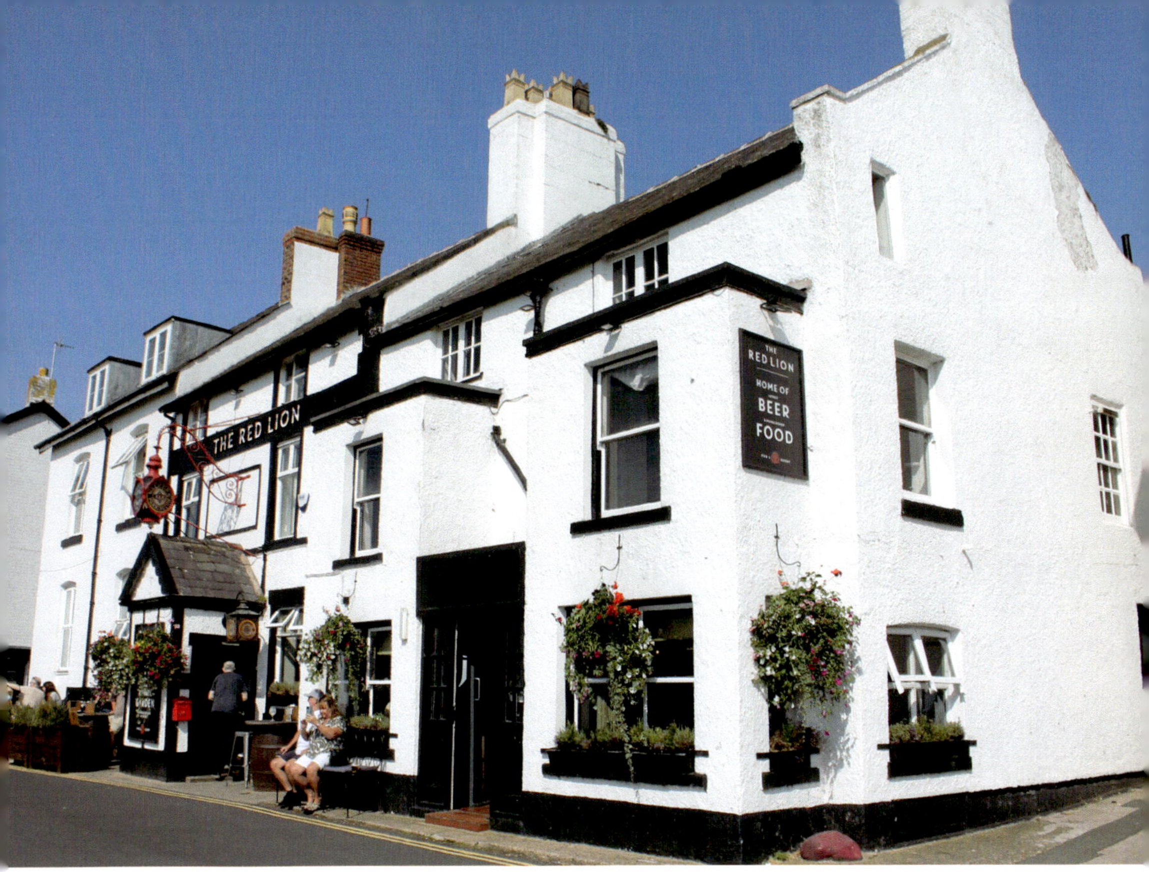

The Red Lion at Parkgate in 2024.

In earlier years additional income would often have been provided by an interest in smuggling but if that did not suit, further dubious income could be achieved by sending false fair weather messages through to Chester in the hope of enticing travellers to Ireland up to Parkgate where they would have to reside in the local inns waiting for a genuine fair wind. A disgruntled traveller wrote of his anger at having been duped into one of the local inns under false pretences and being made 'to lie under the lash of their long bills'. With the decline of Parkgate as a port due to the gradual silting up of the Dee, The Red Lion was one of the few to survive into the twentieth century, and actually expanding its premises in 1934 when it took over the Clondarf Café next door (previously the post office) and incorporated it into the pub.

A pleasurable experience awaits the visitor to The Red Lion nowadays, over and above the view over to the Clwydian mountain range, beginning with the magnificent Walkers of Warrington lamp hanging proudly outside the pub, one of only two still in existence but once seen at nearly all of Walkers outlets. Refurbished in 2021 but still retaining much of the original ambience, the pub offers a wide range of real ales and wines along with the usual lagers and spirits. Regular music nights are held including the ever-popular Rigsbys Cat, still rocking after forty years, along with quiz nights and specials throughout the year.

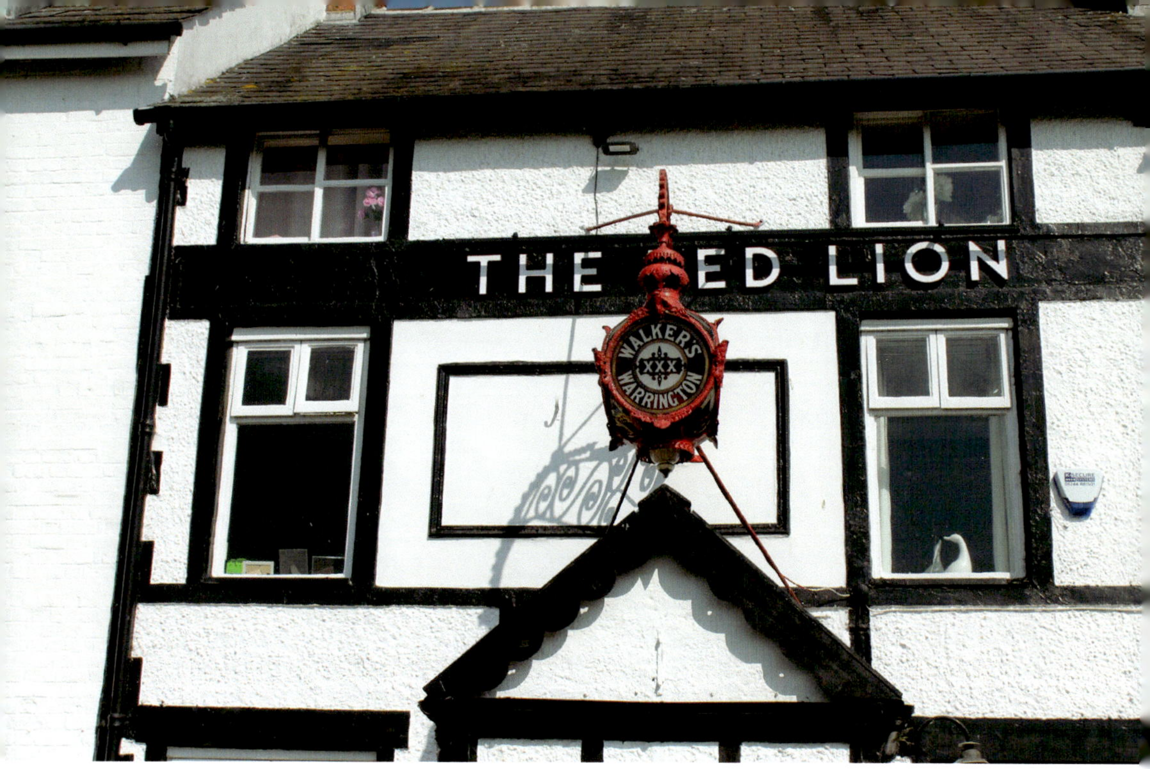

The original Walkers Warrington Ales sign.

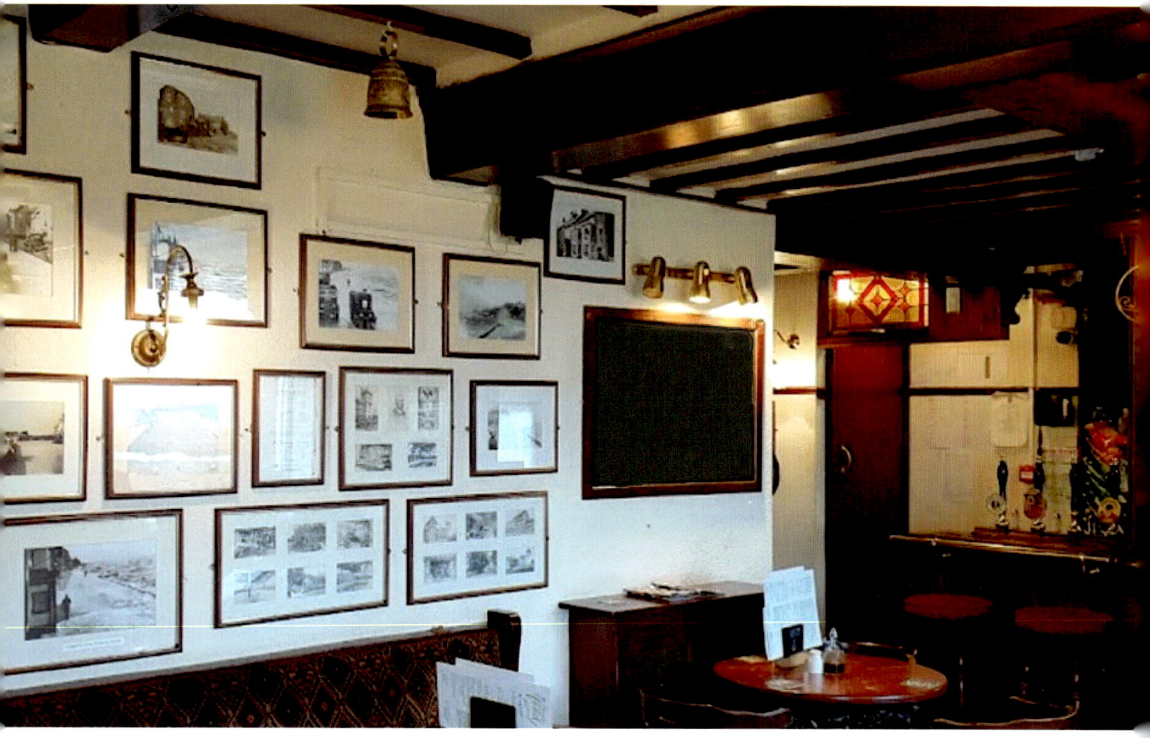

The left-hand lounge in The Red Lion.

21. The Seven Stars, Thornton Hough

The village of Thornton Hough was mentioned in the Domesday Book as Torintone. Its present name came about when the daughter of Roger de Thornton, a major landowner during the reign of Edward II, married Richard de Hughe. Thornton Hough, however, is synonymous with William Lever, Viscount Leverhulme, through his major contribution to the infrastructure of the village during the late nineteenth century. His major works in the area include the magnificent Romanesque church of St George, the village smithy, moved from its original site when the church was built, the Liberal Club and shops, together with picturesque cottages for his workforce and grander mansions dotted around the outskirts for members of his family. His was not, however, the only substantial presence as a Huddersfield textile manufacturer named Joseph Hirst had been busy two decades before, building All Saints Church and the adjacent vicarage, along with Wilshaw Terrace to the north, all in his trademark rock-faced stone.

The Seven Stars pub predates all this feverish activity as there has been an alehouse on the present site since at least 1561 and the present building was there before Hirst arrived in the 1860s. The pub has been the only licensed premises in the village since its one and only rival named The Rising Sun in Clatterbridge Road closed for good in 1864, although the building lived on as Rising Sun Cottage. The fabric of The Seven Stars has

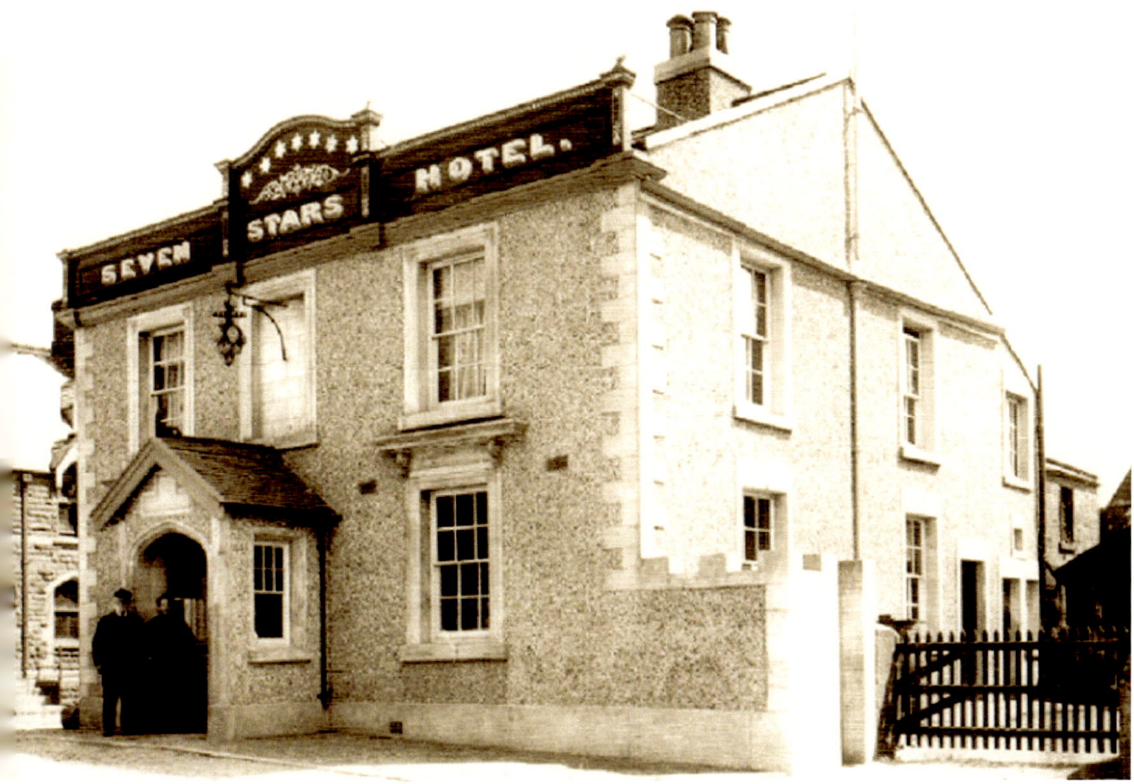

An early view of The Seven Stars, *c.* 1890.

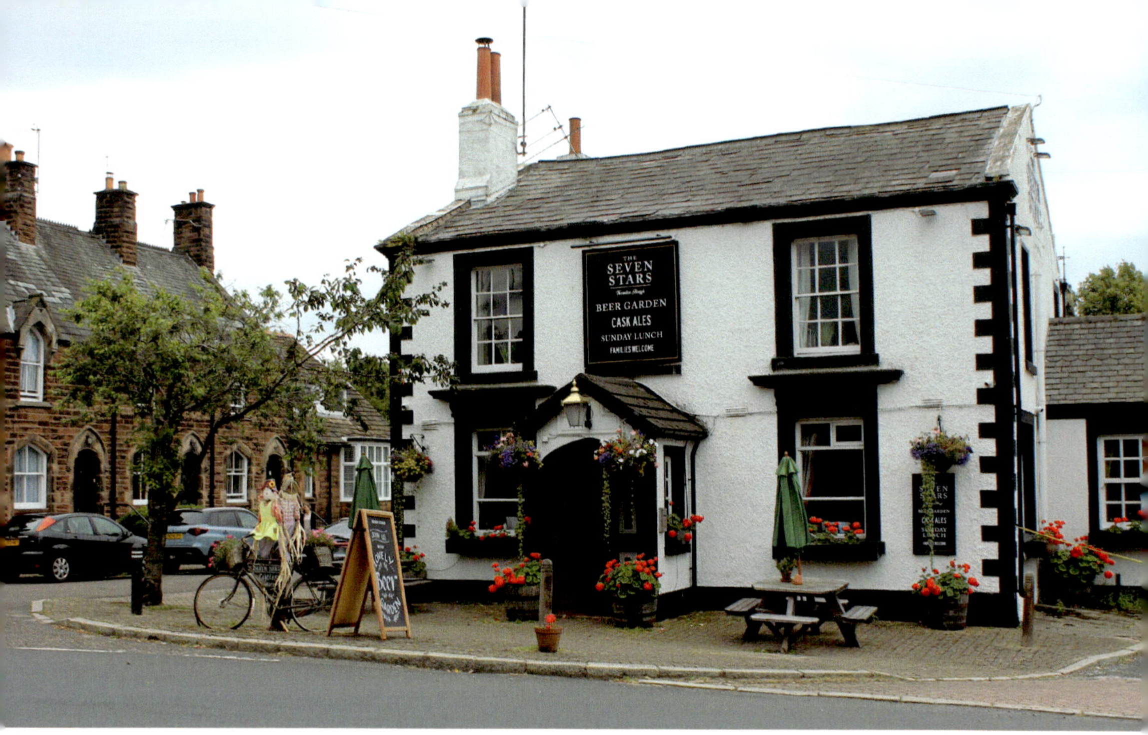

The Seven Stars in 2024.

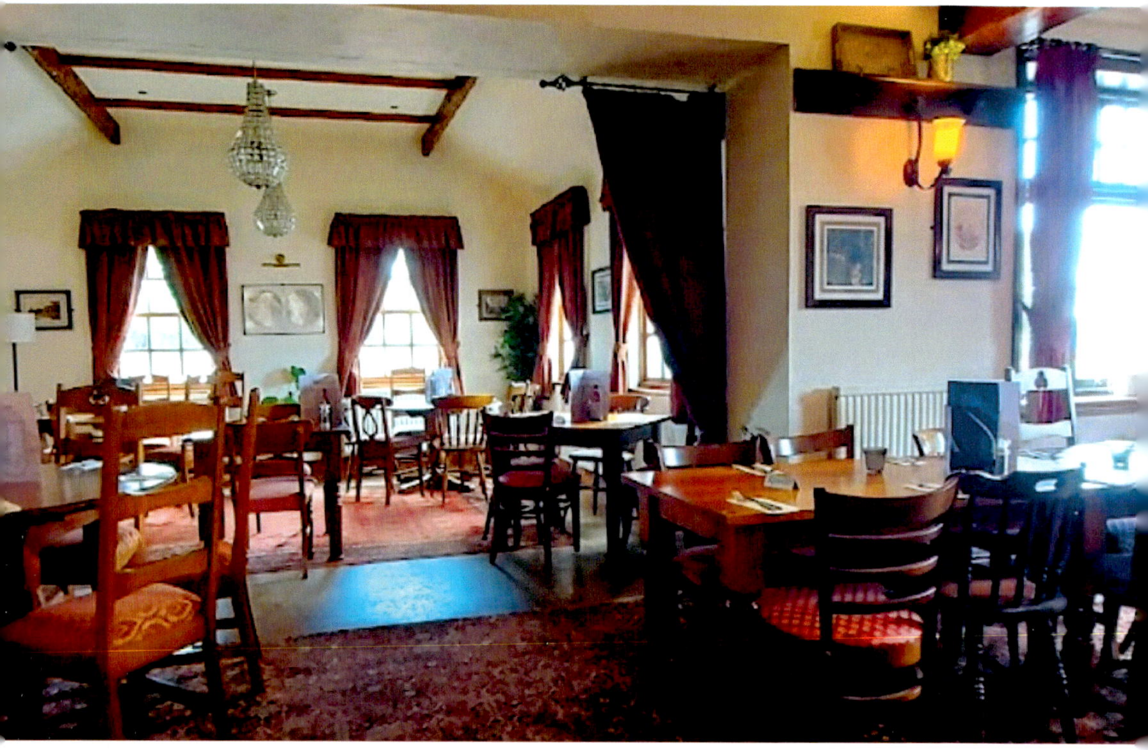

Part of the large dining area at The Seven Stars.

changed little over the years, although it did receive an overdue facelift in 1881 when it gained a smarter looking porch, decorative quoins on the corners and a showy name board above the cornice. The pub was also expanded into the cottages, which once stood in Church Road, appropriately named the Star Cottages. The proprietor at this time was one Thomas Cleworth, who paid £70 per annum for the pub, plus stables, coach house, garden and the three cottages which became part of the premises. It all appears to be a bit of a bargain. He also rented a weighbridge, which was sited in what is now Church Road, an additional source of income popular at the time, at least on Wirral. This facility was finally removed in 1944, taken away possibly as part of the war effort.

The name of the pub is rooted in England's agricultural tradition, which may at first seem odd for such an astrologically sounding appellation, until one realises that the seven stars are representative of Ursa Major, commonly known as the Plough. The Seven Stars is the most popular name for a pub in Britain that is not related to any form of heraldry, and the fifth most popular overall. Most of the pubs so named would have been situated near to where the community plough would have been located and are therefore more likely to be found in rural areas to this day. The pub today is a free house selling beer from the nearby Brimstage Brewery and has retained much of its traditional charm internally, as well as boasting a large outside drinking area.

22. The Wheatsheaf, Raby

Known locally just as The Thatch, the Wheatsheaf Inn has a strong claim for the title of oldest pub in Wirral. Rebuilt after a fire in 1611, it may well have been a licensed premises even before then. The fire gave rise to stories of a spectral figure who has haunted the inn ever since. The legend asserts that a woman called Charlotte died in the conflagration and her ghost continues to appear in the inn and outside in the courtyard. A young women in an 'umbrella dress' has been seen reflected in a mirror, footprints have appeared in a recently mopped floor when no one but the cleaner was around, and she has even been known to move things around, although unlike most poltergeists, she is considered to be a rather friendly spirit.

Detailed records relating to the Wheatsheaf only really begin in 1861 when the local Trade Directory records William Ellison as the licensee. It also states that the pub was a free house owned by the Earl of Shrewsbury, who owned vast tracts of Wirral at the time. The Register of Licensed Houses noted that it had one bed for travellers and catering facilities for several more. This would have been of interest to the many who travelled from Parkgate and Neston across to Birkenhead and over to Liverpool on the early ferries. The interior of the pub has changed little over the years, having fortuitously avoided the attentions of the ghastly 'improvers' who have ruined so many other fine inns. CAMRA have awarded it a two-star rating, classed as 'a pub interior of very special national historic interest'. It goes on to describe it as 'a timber-framed building with a thatched roof and bearing a datestone of 1611'. The principal interest lies, however, in the tall-backed settles in the snug area, which are arranged around a large wooden table adjacent to a substantial brick fireplace. It is incredibly warm

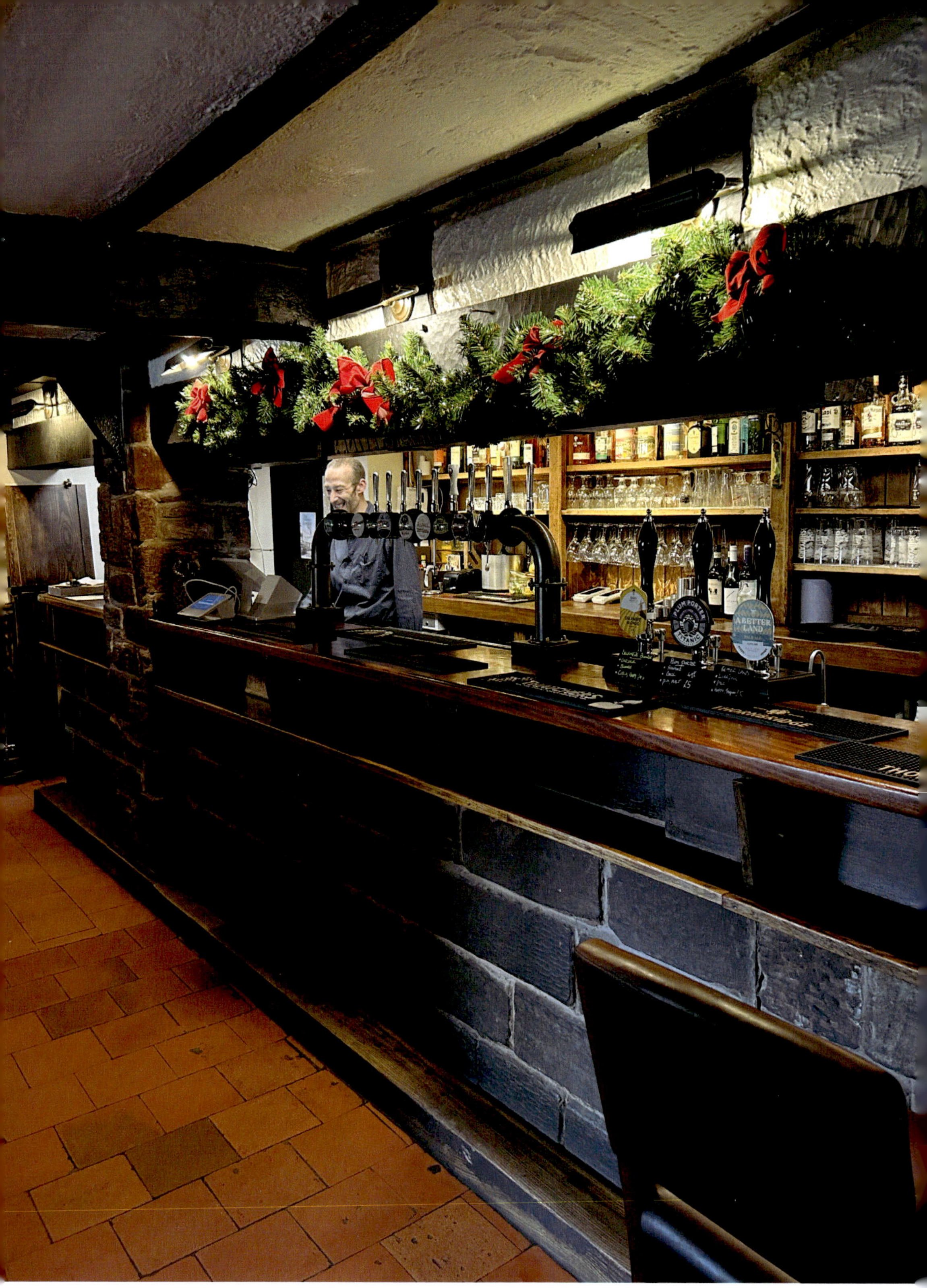

The main bar area at The Wheatsheaf.

and cosy on cold winter days after a brisk walk along one of the many pathways surrounding the inn – in fact it can get a bit too hot at times. One of the settles has glazed panels above, whilst the other has a fielded wooden panel. Only around a dozen other pubs have managed to retain their original settles, including a couple in nearby Derbyshire.

Pubs that are located away from centres of population always need to provide a reason for customers to patronise their premises and The Wheatsheaf has several. In addition to its historical interest and resident ghost, it provides a large selection of real ales and excellent pub food. To cater for customers who wish to have a sit-down meal, there is also a sizeable restaurant area, which has been created by converting an old shippon into The Cow Shed Restaurant, thankfully not to the detriment of the original pub. There are also two large outside drinking areas for use in the warmer weather and a few benches to the front where you can enjoy your pint and watch the world go by.

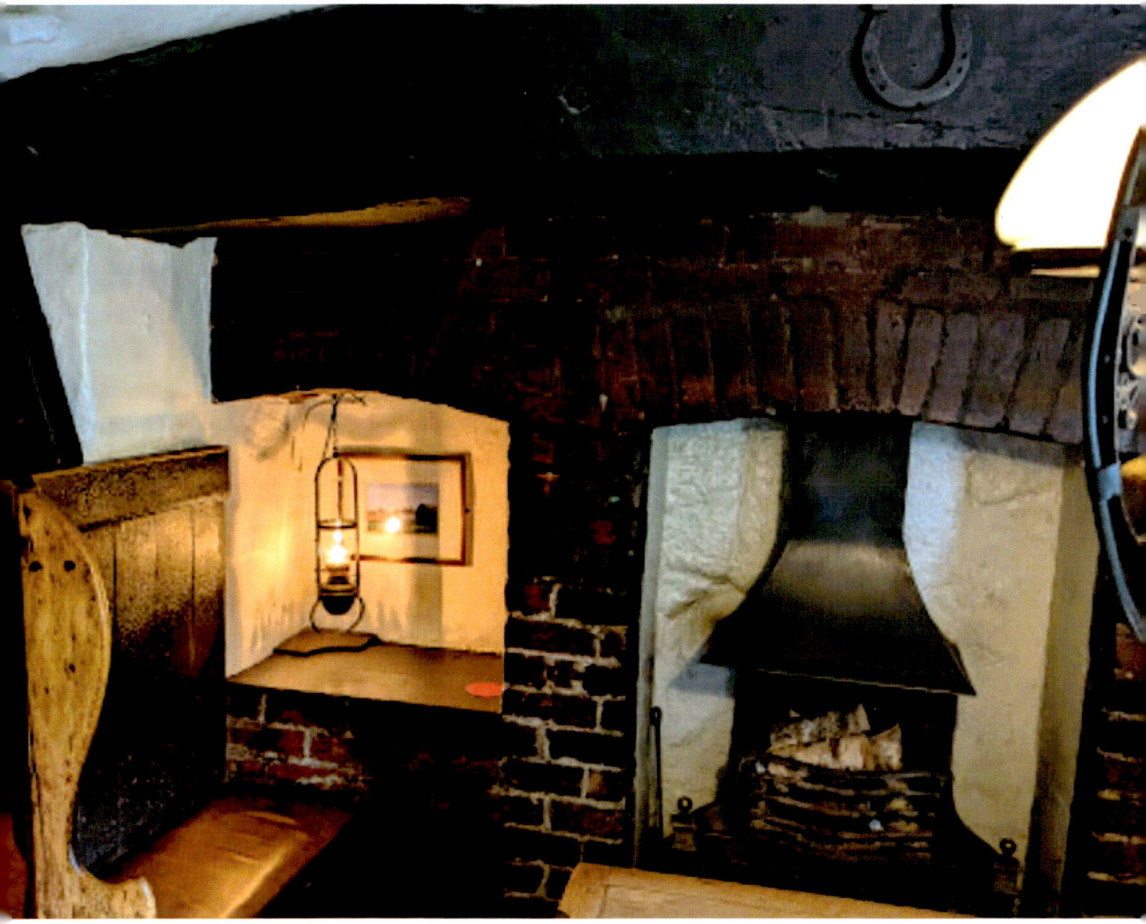

Old settle and cosy fireplace in The Thatch.

23. The Bridge Inn, Port Sunlight

Famous the world over, Port Sunlight Model Village was the brainchild of William Hesketh Lever, designed to both house and educate his workforce in the strict moral values he lived by. His laudable profit-sharing scheme was invested in the village rather than to the workforce directly, making his views crystal clear when he said 'It would not do you much good if you send it down your throat in the form of bottles of whisky, bags of sweets, or fat geese at Christmas. On the other hand if you leave the money with me, I shall use it to provide for you everything that makes life pleasant – nice houses, comfortable homes and healthy recreation'.

This proselytising zeal was extended further into the leisure time of his employees as he built not a pub but a temperance hotel in the centre of the village. He clearly thought the turpitude of his workforce was best addressed by providing uplifting religious and moral guidance through temperance. His workforce clearly had other ideas and to his credit Lever allowed a free vote on whether The Bridge should become licensed for the sale of alcohol, but only if 75 per cent of the villagers voted for it. By the smallest of margins they did indeed vote for it, and halves of sarsaparilla gave way to flagons of foaming ale as The Bridge Inn as we know it was born. Great weight has been given to the fact that Lever allowed women to vote, but this was more likely to have been

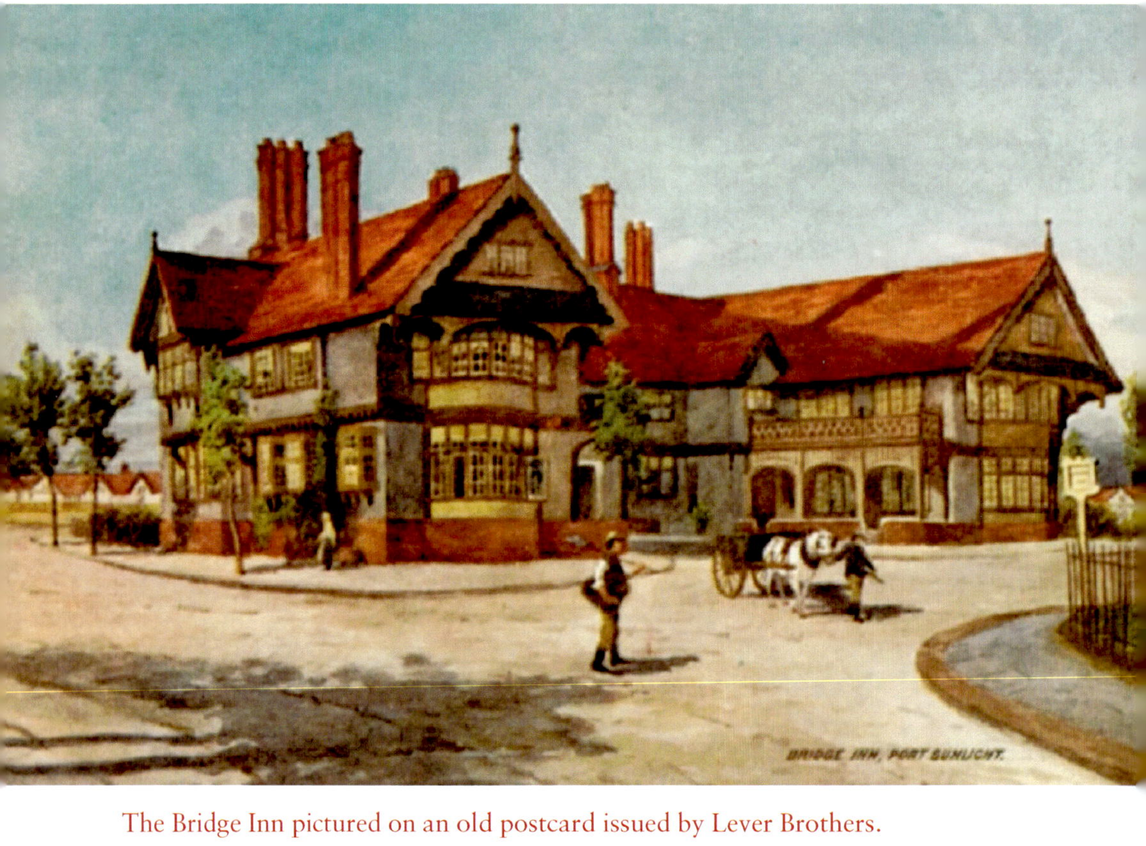

The Bridge Inn pictured on an old postcard issued by Lever Brothers.

a ploy to sway the vote his way as he (wrongly) thought women were more likely to keep the inn dry, rather than an early example of women's suffrage. The pub was given a six-day licence in 1903 but no Sunday opening of course – Lever would have never agreed to that.

The pub was designed to fit in perfectly with the architecture of the rest of the village with half-timbering and a touch of Arts and Crafts about it, looking in fact more Edwardian than Victorian. But why call it The Bridge? The nearest bridge is nearly half a mile away. The answer lies outside, beneath Bolton Road, where the short-lived Victoria Bridge once spanned the largest of the many gulleys that once peppered the landscape before the village was constructed. In 1910 when the creek was filled in there was clearly no need for the bridge and the parapet was removed and the whole bridge buried beneath Bolton Road. One of the foundation stones with the name of the bridge and its construction date has been perfunctorily dumped by the side of the road as an afterthought. The parapet was reused on the New Chester Bridge nearby.

The Bridge boasts large overhanging gables with its U shape with verandas of cross wings enclosing an excellent forecourt, the porch here being a later addition. It was greatly enlarged in 1964 but mercifully it was designed to be in

The Bridge Inn in 2024.

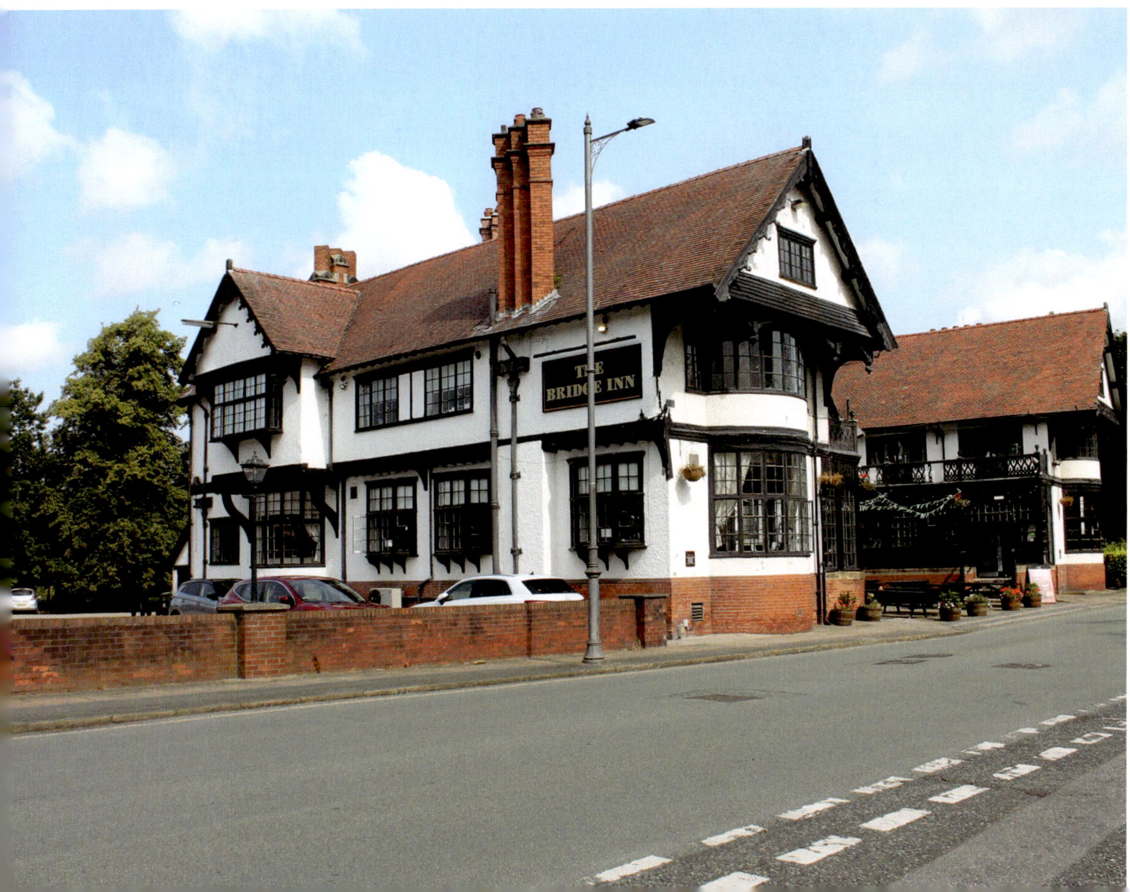

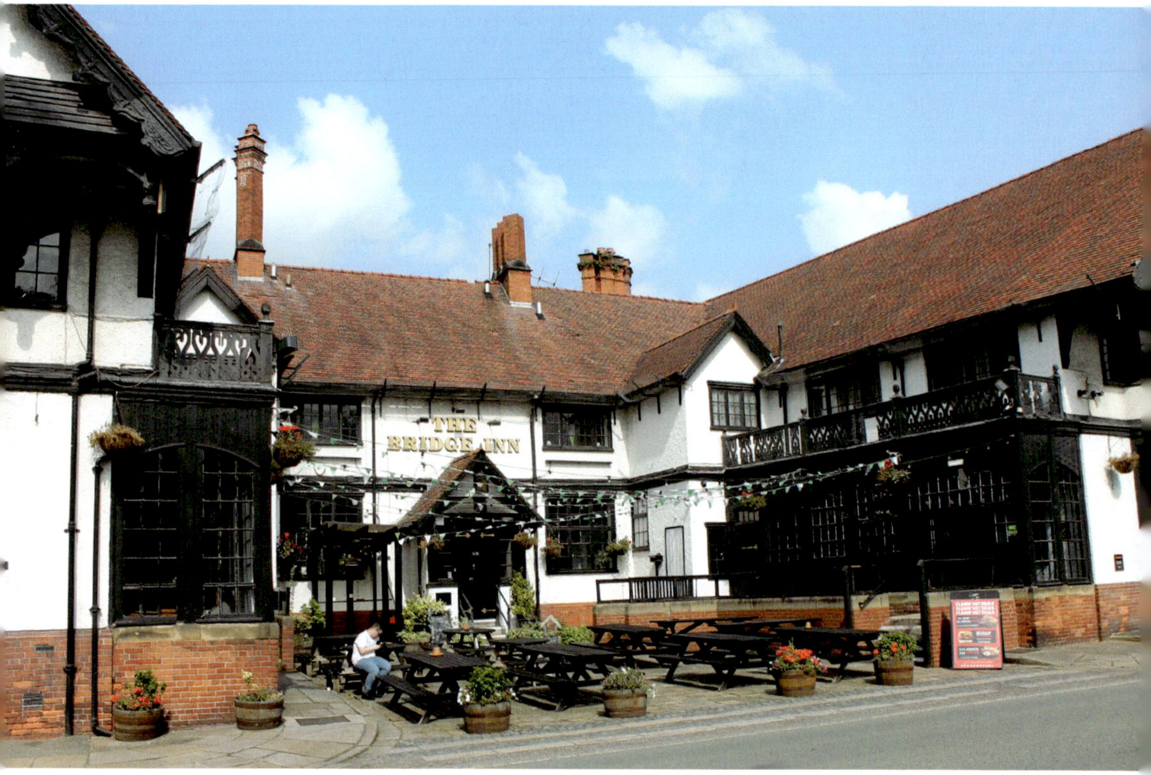

The courtyard area in 2024.

keeping with the pub and the village in general, although the scale is not quite right. However, the removal of many original internal Victorian fittings and their replacement with pseudo-Victorian tat is a matter of regret. Conceived in the ideal of health, purity and sobriety, The Bridge Inn continues to serve the community well.

24. The Bromborough Hotel, Bromborough

Although the pub itself only dates back to 1822, the village in which it lies dates back nearly 1,000 years and can put in a good claim to be the site of one of the most significant battles in English history. Although contested by some historians, most now agree that the Battle of Brunanburgh took place a stone's throw from the pub door and led to the formation of the English nation as we know it. When built, the Bromborough Hotel was called The Mainwaring Arms after the lords of the manor and incumbents of Bromborough Hall, the oldest of many fine mansions in the area. It was to undergo many changes of name throughout the nineteenth century, being known as The Sportsmans Arms in the 1850s, the Pic-Nic Hotel in the 1860s, before settling on its current name in 1896. It was also known colloquially as The Asses Head, an allusion to the rather strange charge of a donkey above the gules and or mantling and helm on the Mainwaring families coat of arms.

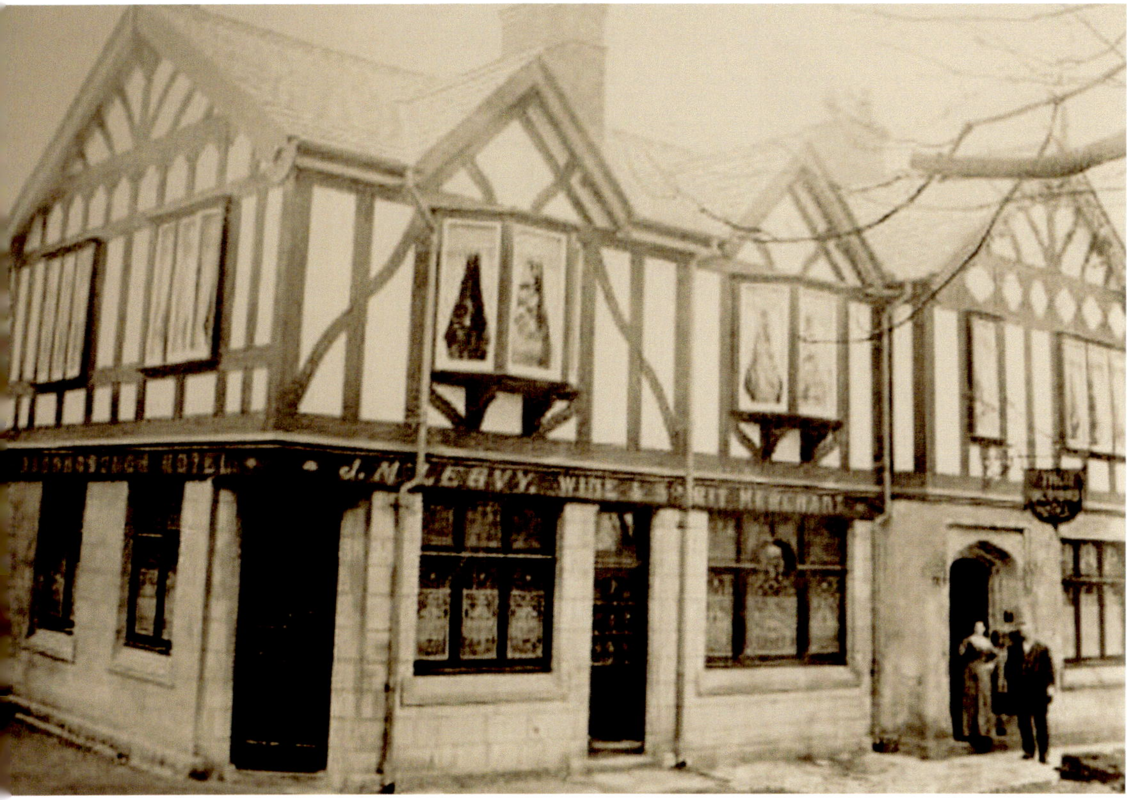

Above: The Bromborough Hotel pictured on an old postcard, *c.* 1910.

Below: The Bromborough Hotel in 2024.

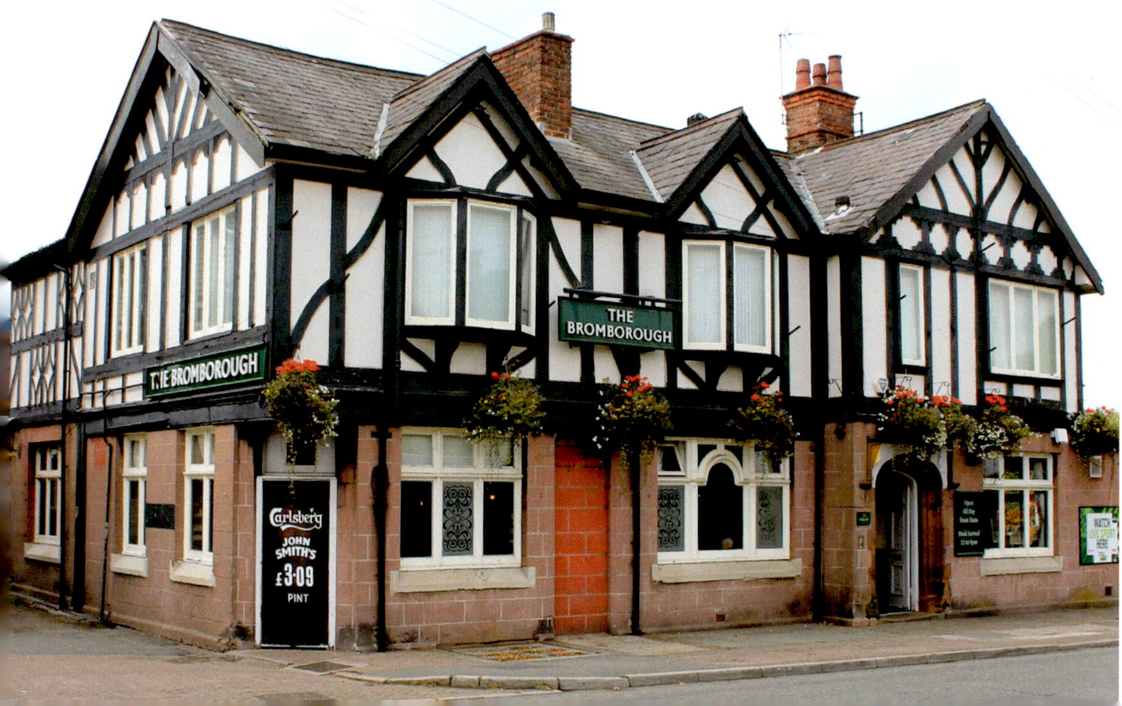

The location of the pub turned out to be very fortuitous as soon after its construction a new turnpike road was built linking Bromborough initially to Tranmere Ferry and later to Woodside Ferry, one of Thomas Brassey's largest local undertakings. This later became part of the A41 and, coupled with the building of the Chester to Birkenhead Railway, which opened in 1840, enabled wealthy Liverpool merchants to choose Wirral as a place to make their homes, the beginning of the commuter belt on the eastern coast of Wirral. Many fine mansions were built in the vicinity of the Bromborough Arms such as Plymyard House, Mensall House, Bankdale and Woodslea House, and whilst the merchants themselves would probably not have patronised the pub, the masses of servants, gardeners and sundry other staff certainly would have popped in during their limited time off.

Major alterations were made to the building in 1909 when it was decided to widen the road outside. This process often sounded the death knell of many a fine building but luckily the pub was spared and they managed to widen the road on the eastern side instead. It has to be said that the old building was rather plain, of brick with three gables facing the road and fancy bargeboards, a terracotta string course and that's about it in the way of decoration. The alterations managed to retain the three gables with their façades being tricked out in half-timbering. Unfortunately the replacement bargeboards lost their swagger.

What the new road had given to the Bromborough Hotel was to be taken away in the 1930s when the Bromborough Bypass was constructed to the east of the pub, taking away much of the passing trade and, worse still, led to the destruction of Bromborough Hall and the historic White Row, a series of preposterously picturesque cottages which also had the misfortune to lie in the path of the new road. The pub now sits in the centre of the Bromborough Village Conservation Area, created in July 1982 and' as stated in the Conservation Report, 'visually punctuates the streetscape and marks the transition from Stanhope House to the more commercial area of Bromborough'.

The pub is deceptively large inside and is separated into a dining area, a sports screen area and a nice beer garden outside. It is now owned by the ubiquitous Greene King retail and brewing empire with its house beers and wines. Dog walkers may also be interested to know that the pub is dog friendly as long as they behave themselves (the dogs and the owners).

25. The White Lion, Childer Thornton

As you drive out of Little Sutton along the A41 towards Junction 5 of the M53, tucked in between is the little-known village of Childer Thornton, surrounded by fields and very rural by Ellesmere Port standards. Its main attraction from an architectural point of view is undoubtably the magnificent church of St Paul, possibly the finest church in Wirral. Tucked around the back, however, on the opposite side of the main road is the White Lion, steeped in history and still boasting a village pub atmosphere where a friendly greeting is guaranteed. Dating back to 1724, it was originally a homestead and became a pub around 1830 when a change in the law allowed such residences to sell beer to the general public.

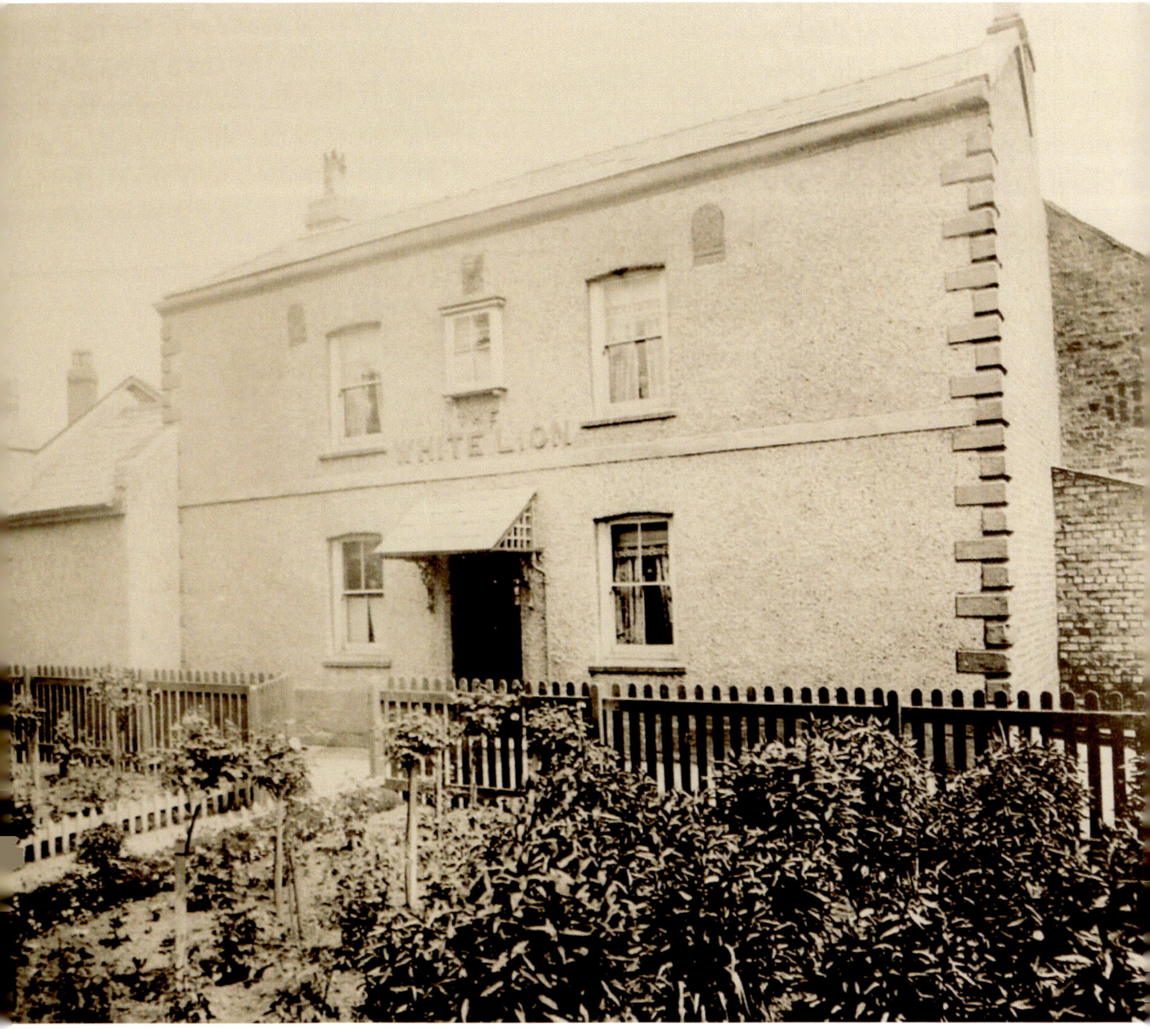

The White Lion at Childer Thornton in 1900.

There are several small, atmospheric rooms within and a small dining area at the rear where excellent meals can be enjoyed. The car park at the rear backs on to the original stables, which provided accommodation for our four-legged friends before the advent of the internal combustion engine.

Life around these parts was not always quite so idyllic as the story of the Riot of Childer Thornton, outlined in a framed piece at the bar, attests. Some 180 years ago the place was awash with workers attracted to the area by the building of the Chester to Birkenhead Railway. The navvies who worked on the line consisted of English and Irish workers who by and large got on well with each other. This was until one fateful day in 1839 when an English contractor insisted on using only English navvies for a particular job. This did not go down well with the Irishmen of course and unfortunately violence ensued. Mass brawls broke out with pickaxe handles, shovels, bludgeons and

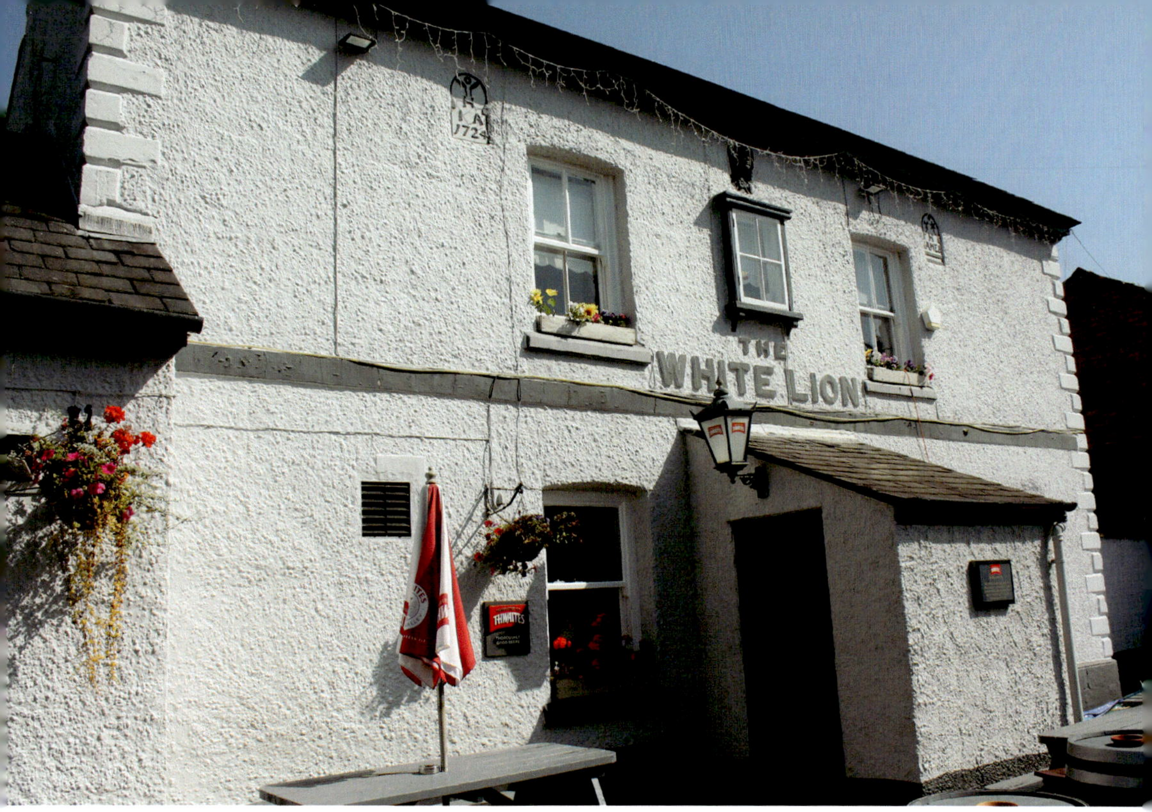

Above: The White Lion in 2024.

Below: View from the bar in The White Lion.

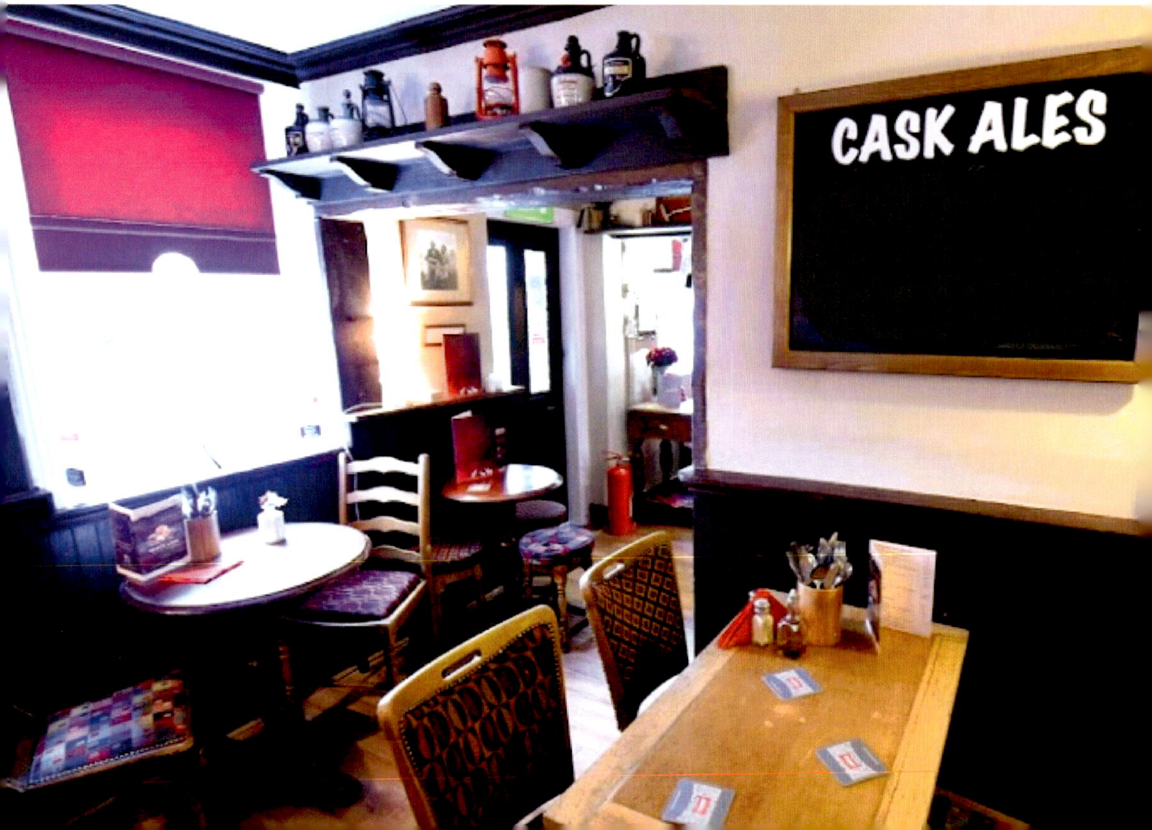

whatever else came to hand. The English soon lost the battle and the Irishmen ran riot for the next four days, taking over the local pubs including the White Lion and drinking it dry. Order was not restored until a contingent of infantry from the nearby Chester Barracks arrived, arresting the ringleaders and cracking open a few heads.

Tranquillity was restored to the area and it returned to its somnolent normality. Patrons of the White Lion can still enjoy a quiet drink here today, either in the pub or outside in the excellent beer garden, untroubled by warring hordes of navvies.

26. The Eastham Ferry

Eastham is one of the oldest villages in Wirral but it was to the north of the original village that attention was turned to at the beginning of the nineteenth century when the development of the Birkenhead to Chester Railway and the opening of the ferry from Liverpool to Eastham had greatly increased the volume of travellers through the area. Sir William Stanley was fortunate enough to own the ferry and most of the land hereabouts and as with most Victorian landowners, he realised the potential to make more money for himself by developing the land adjacent to the ferry. He built a large hotel in 1843 just south of the ferry terminal and modestly called it The Stanley Arms. It soon became known as The Eastham Ferry Hotel and remains so to this day.

Sir William developed a large part of the estate as pleasure gardens as they were demurely called in the Victorian era, landscaped gardens of rhododendron and azalea,

The Eastham Ferry Hotel from an old postcard.

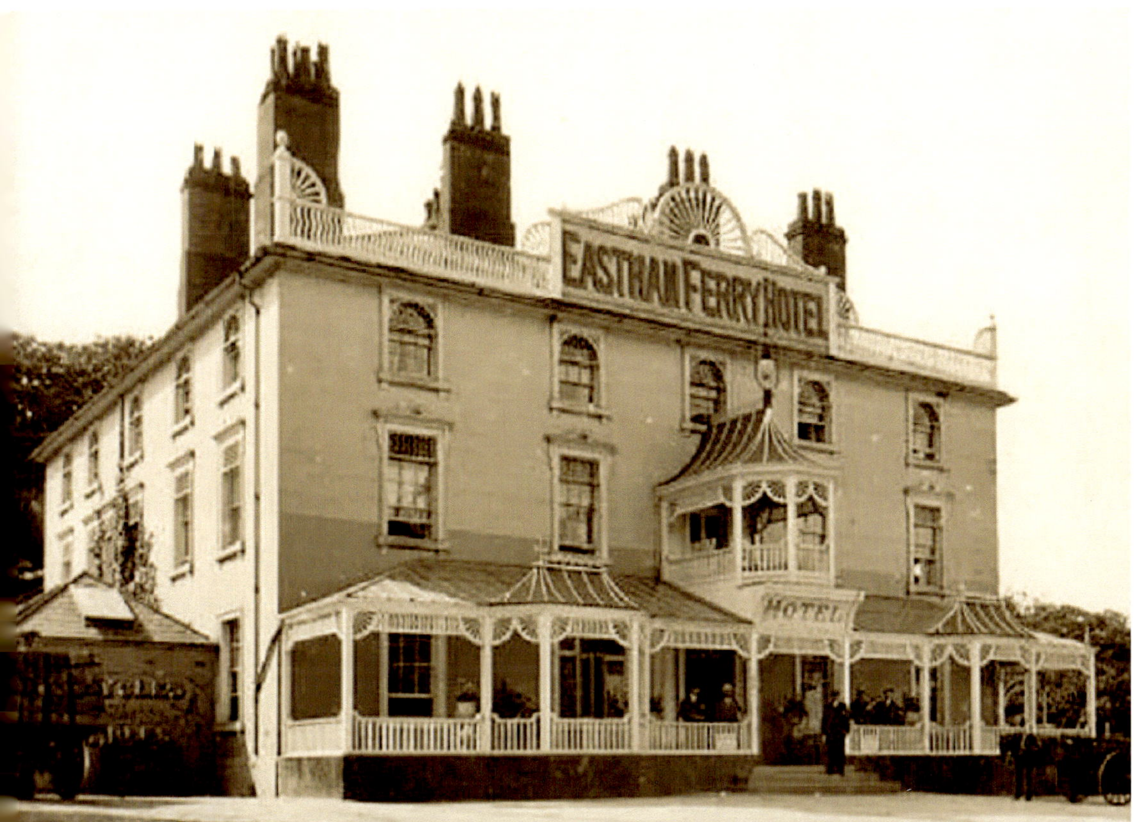

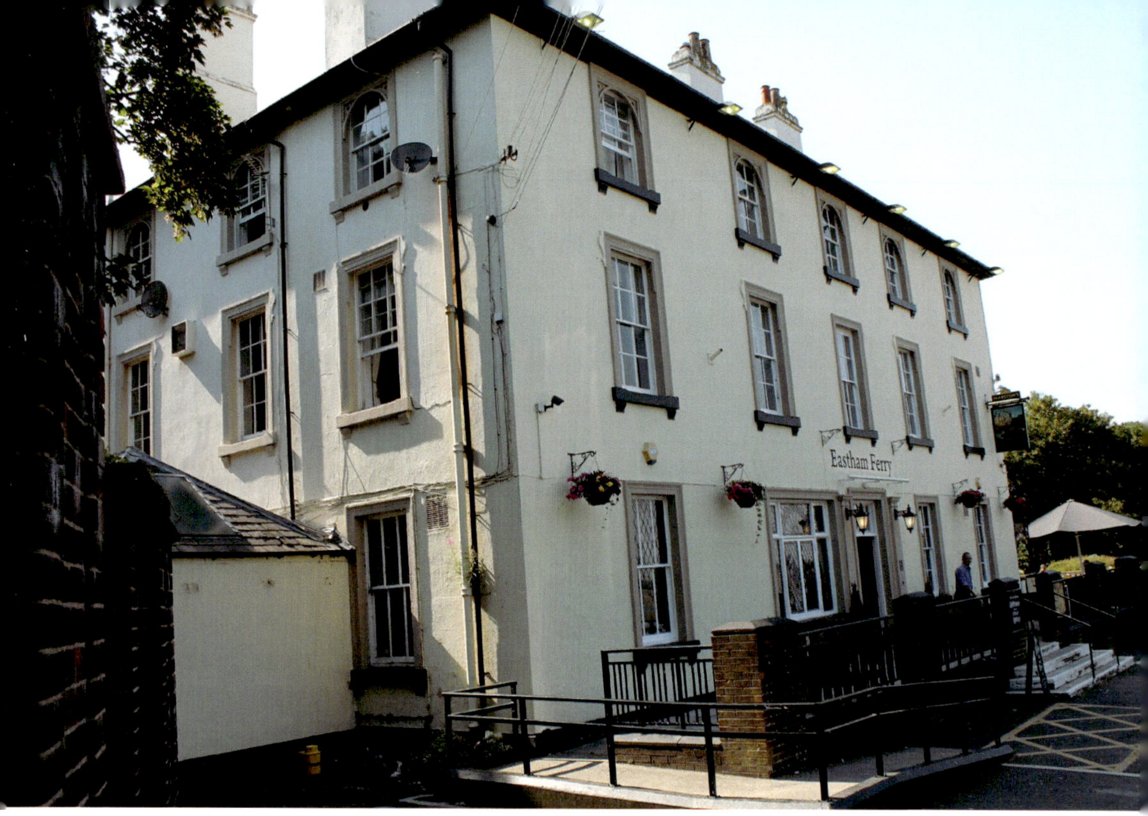

The Eastham Ferry Hotel today.

ornamental trees and fountains and a zoological garden with bears, lions, monkeys and antelopes – one can almost picture wildebeest sweeping majestically across the plain and The Hanging Gardens of Babylon but that was for another time. An open-air stage was constructed along with tearooms, a bandstand, ballroom, boating lake, water chute, loop-the-loop ride and Charles Blondin with his tightrope walking stunts, oftentimes with a willing or not so willing spectator squashed into a wheelbarrow for good measure. It became known as the Richmond of the Mersey but I can't imagine the one in Surrey being this much fun. The Victorians didn't do things by halves when it came to entertaining the great British public.

Perhaps the greatest achievement was the building of the Jubilee Arch adjacent to The Eastham Ferry Hotel, a copy of the Marble Arch in London and built to commemorate the Diamond Jubilee of Queen Victoria in 1897. This was sadly demolished in the 1930s as the council deemed it unsafe, although they changed their minds after it was destroyed – *quelle surprise*.

Just after the Jubilee Arch was constructed the hotel gained a magnificent ornamental balcony, which gave patrons a peerless view across the Mersey with unrivalled views of the shipping on the river. This was later destroyed despite the building having listed status. An advertisement from the 1890s gives an idea of the luxurious nature of the hotel at this time: 'Charmingly situated with its beautiful grounds and gardens facing the River Mersey, near the entrance to the Ship Canal and replete with all modern requirements. Eleven bedrooms all fitted with hot and cold water and gas fires.' In the

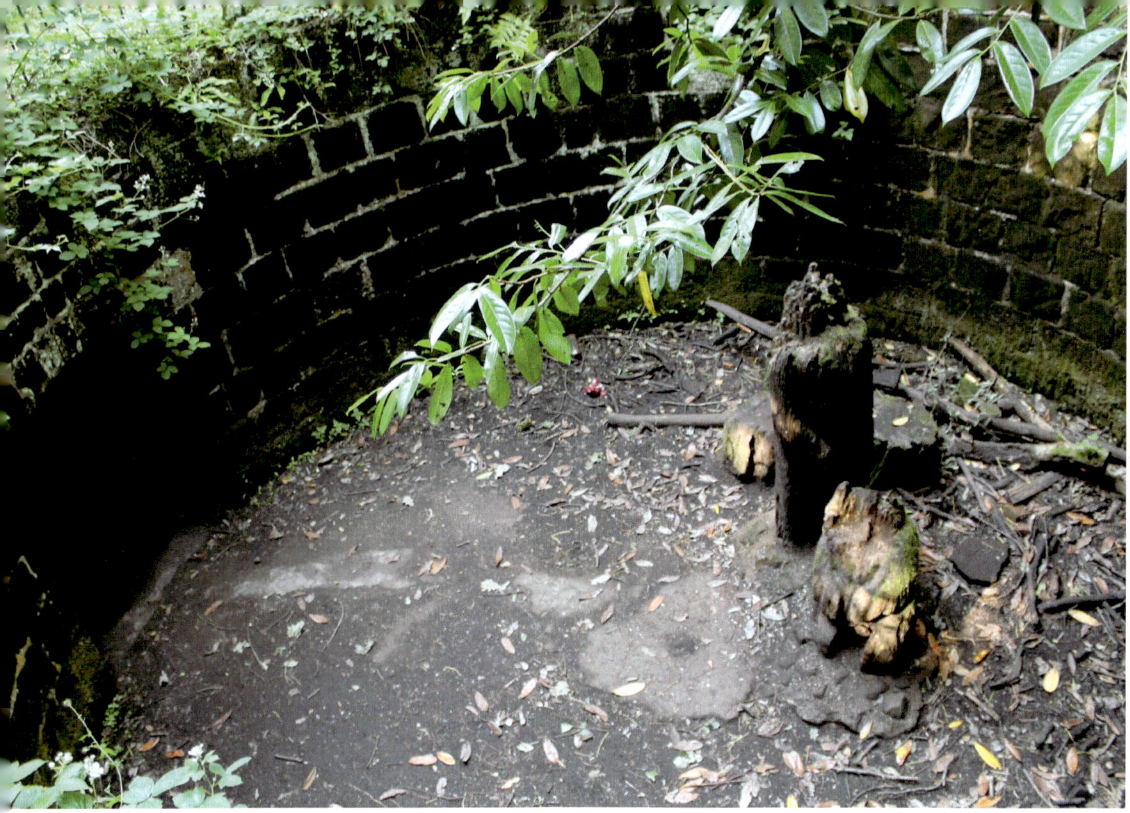

The bear pit in Eastham Country Park.

days when travellers still arrived by horse or horse-driven vehicles the fact that the hotel had stabling for thirty horses would certainly have been another useful amenity. It was not uncommon for the hotel to cater for around 1,000 people in a single day.

If the late 1800s were the apogee for the area, the twentieth century was not so kind to The Eastham Ferry and its environs, with the ferry service to Liverpool ceasing in 1929 and the landing stage and pier being demolished in 1935. The Jubilee Arch came down in 1930 and the wildlife moved to pastures new. Blondin was to die quietly in his house in Ealing. There is still plenty of evidence of the headier days of Eastham however, as opposite the hotel the ticket office for the ferry remains and the fountains, part of the ornamental gardens and even the bear pit can still be seen in the woods behind the hotel.

27. The Harp, Little Neston

Why would anyone want to build a pub in such an isolated location, on the windswept west Wirral coast, far from any road and untroubled by any passing trade? The answer lies 30 feet below the pub and out into the estuary where men, women and even children toiled in the semi-darkness in horrendous conditions to eke out an existence bringing coal up to feed the developing Industrial Revolution and its insatiable demand for steam.

The first mine was carved out in 1778 and all these thirsty miners required somewhere to slake their thirst after an extremely long shift, particularly if the alternative was to return directly to their 'most miserable mass of hovels'. In light of this one enterprising individual converted three existing cottages into one in 1780 and obtained a beer licence

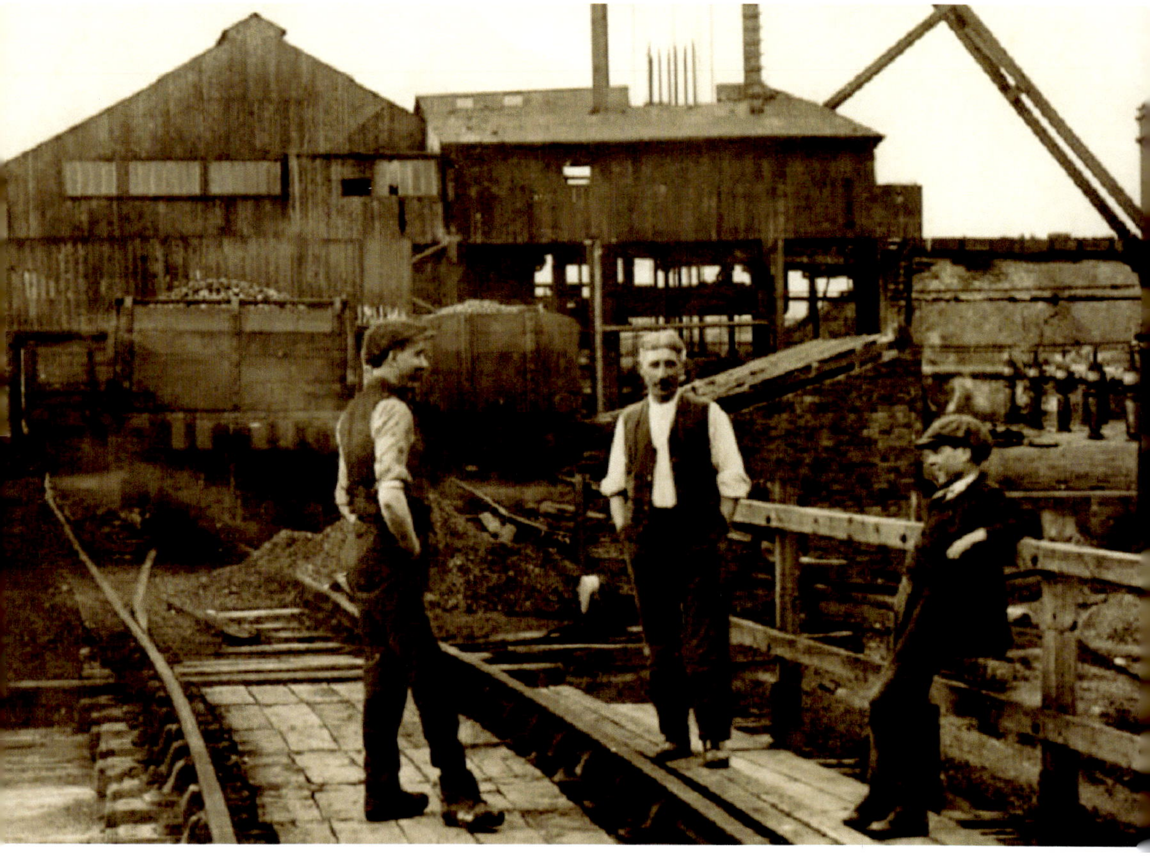

Miners outside the old Neston Coal Pit.

to open it as a pub. The premises became known as The Welsh Harp, adopted from a nickname given to the premises by the large contingent of Welsh miners who drank there. With two coal shafts being opened by 1820 a bitter rivalry built up between miners from the two pits who were happy to flood or even blow up each other's workings. As The Harp was the only pub for miles around, these local rivalries amongst the miners were confined to their day job, with the pub considered neutral ground. With only two small rooms, the miners utilised the small public bar to the left of the entrance whilst the managers drank in the lounge. The pub retains this arrangement to the present day, so if you are feeling particularly managerial turn right at the front door.

In 1875 the then owners, Birkenhead Brewery, applied to pull The Harp down and build a larger pub on the land, but only if they could obtain a full licence. Luckily this was not granted and the pub was saved for posterity. Nothing much changed over the ensuing years, at least not above ground, but permission was sought and granted by the Wirral Colliery Company to construct two roads beneath the pub to convey coal by underground rail from the coal face under The Dee, at a royalty of £3 per annum.

Limekilns and brickmaking added to the industrial milieu with the area employing over 300 people by the 1920s. A small contingent of waterfowlers also patronised the pub, as noted by the enormous punt gun that used to grace the wall of the public bar. All this was gone by the 1950s, however, with the colliery having closed in 1927 and the other industries gradually declining over time. Nowadays it is walkers and twitchers, dog owners and motorists who make up the clientele, seeking out the peerless ales or view. Having remained unchanged for so many years, The Harp offers basic amenities at reasonable prices – no juke boxes or gaming machines, no TVs or other distractions, just an old traditional pub atmosphere and a cracking location, somewhere to relax and escape the madding crowd for an hour or so, especially on a warm summer's evening.

28. The Olde Red Lion, Little Sutton

There has been a hostelry of some kind on or near to the site of the present Olde Red Lion for hundreds of years. Not surprising really as this area has always been a centre of the community. Previously called The Square, it was the general meeting place for political rallies, annual fairs and latterly the meeting place for the Wirral Harriers foxhunt, organised by Sir Thomas Stanley and his foxhounds. This was a ghastly pastime for toffs that has, by and large, been committed to the dustbin of history. 'The unspeakable in pursuit of the inedible' as Oscar Wilde famously said, ever one for the pithy phrase.

It is perhaps a little surprising that the pub on The Square was not named The Fox and Hounds but The Red Lion, the most popular pub name in Great Britain and one with its historical origins in the fledgling Stuart period. When James I (James VI of Scotland if you are of the sporran sporting persuasion) came to the throne of England in 1603 he decreed that the red lion of Scotland be displayed on all buildings of importance, and being Scottish this of course included the pubs, with many retaining the designation to this day. The version of the Olde Red Lion before the current building was far smaller,

The Red Lion in Little Sutton in 2024.

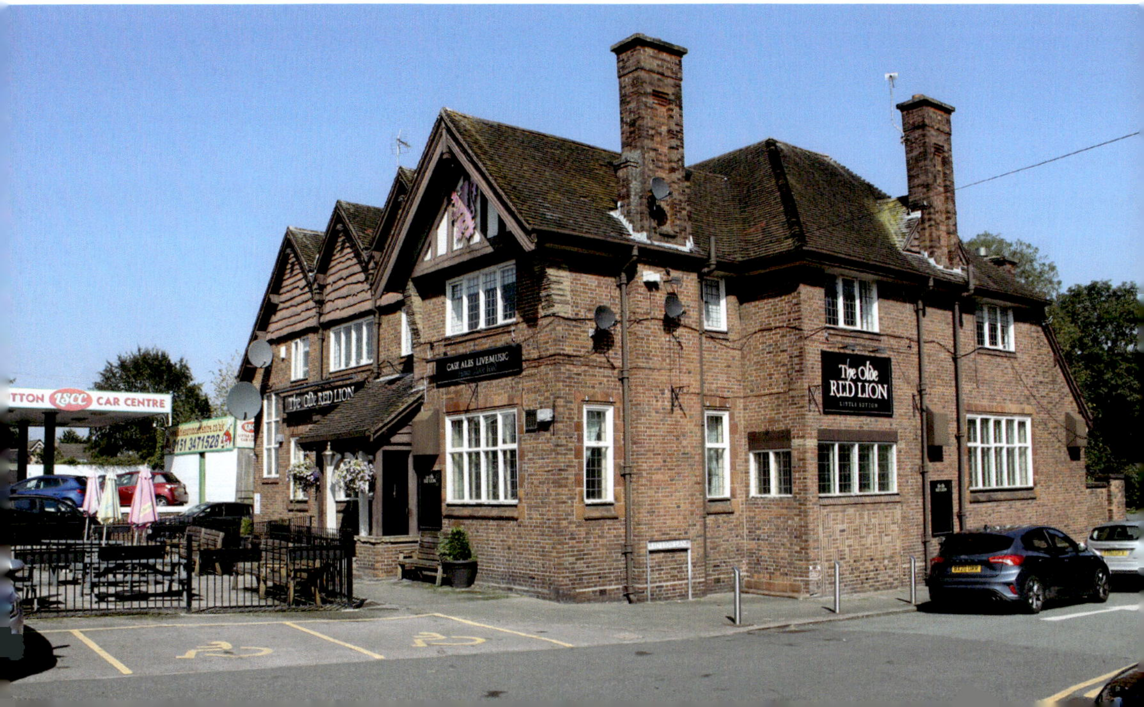

with two main drinking rooms either side of the main door, and the pub name proudly painted on the roof. As a valuable asset the pub was used in 1888 as collateral by the local branch of the Oddfellows Society, who were owners at the time, to raise funds to build eight cottages in the adjacent Red Lion Lane; in fact the pub was known at the time as the Oddfellows Hall or more cruelly as the Cow Shed.

When the Red Lion was taken over by Birkenhead Brewery in 1934 they made the decision to demolish the old pub and build a far bigger one behind, with the licence being swapped over before the old pub was pulled down. As noted earlier this was an odd quirk of the law which had to be followed if the valuable drinks licence was to be retained. The new pub was indeed far bigger, with three weatherboarded and one half-timbered gable facing the road, constructed rather strangely in an old-fashioned Flemish Bond. The site of the old pub now forms part of the drinking area to the front. A nice touch, which is mostly missed by patrons, is a delightfully carved red lion tucked away above a private entrance to the left.

The new pub has proved a popular venue in the village, with The Olde Red Lion being ably run by Jackie and Andy Fadden for nearly twenty years before their recent retirement/jolly to Mexico. It regularly attracts many of the top local musical acts, many of whom bring their own loyal following along. Although it is a big pub, the Faddens promoted a warm, friendly atmosphere – long may it continue.

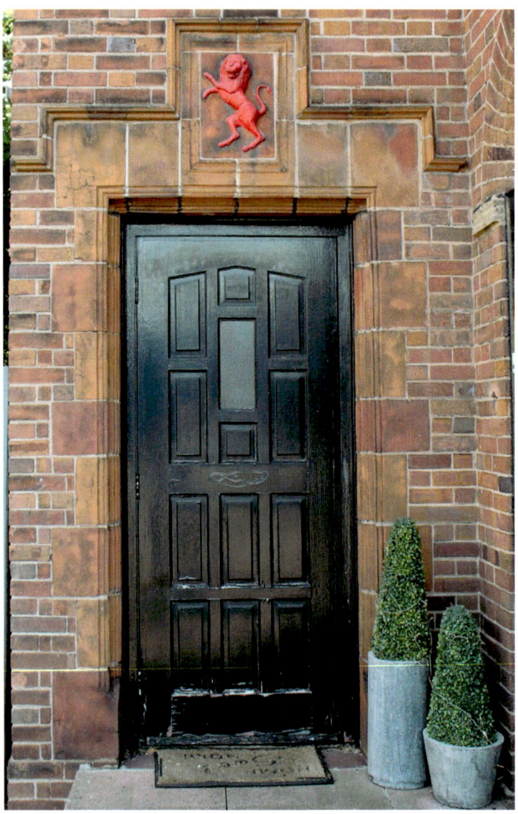

The red lion rampant above a side door at the Red Lion.

Former Pubs

Wirral pubs have continued to close at an alarming rate. The double whammy of Covid and a cost-of-living crisis exacerbated an already downward trend. However, some of these buildings remain and, although being repurposed into flats, restaurants and various other guises, have often left clues as to their original purpose, frequently in the form of lettering in stone which has been left on the facia during conversion. The following chapter contains examples of some of these ghost pubs. There are many more out there to discover if you know where to look or are of a certain age and have a good memory.

29. The Little Brighton, New Brighton

Built around 1840 for the Argyle Brewery in Birkenhead, the pub was initially named The Chequers until it was bought by Birkenhead Brewery, who renamed it as The Little Brighton, although the area is actually called Upper Brighton. The nickname it

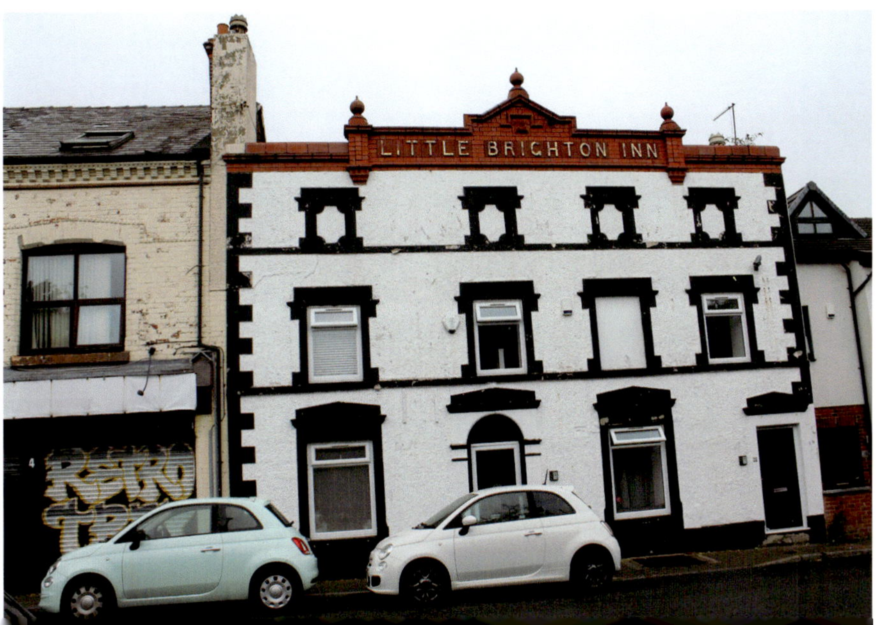

The Little Brighton after conversion into flats.

retained right through to its closure in 2012 was 'The Ginnie', which dates way back to the 1850s when the massively popular Swedish opera singer Johanna Maria Lind reportedly stayed at the inn whilst performing in Liverpool.

There was a large villa located next to the pub, but this was pulled down in the 1990s, leaving a large empty area behind a high sandstone wall. Planning permission was eventually given to construct nine houses on the site of the villa and also incorporating The Little Brighton. The pub is still instantly recognisable as the complete façade has been retained, including the excellent lettering on the facia above, and the fine windows and doors with their broad Victorian drip moulds and sills. It is a rare example of what can be done with an old pub, using a little imagination and thought.

30. The Albion Hotel, New Brighton

Possibly built on the directions of the Earls of Derby, the Royal Albion Hotel, as it was originally named, was constructed as part of the massive development of the area by James Atherton and William Rowson in the 1820s and 1830s and formed part of the upper tier of housing which swept down to the shoreline and commanded excellent views of Liverpool and the River Mersey. It was always popular, particularly in the

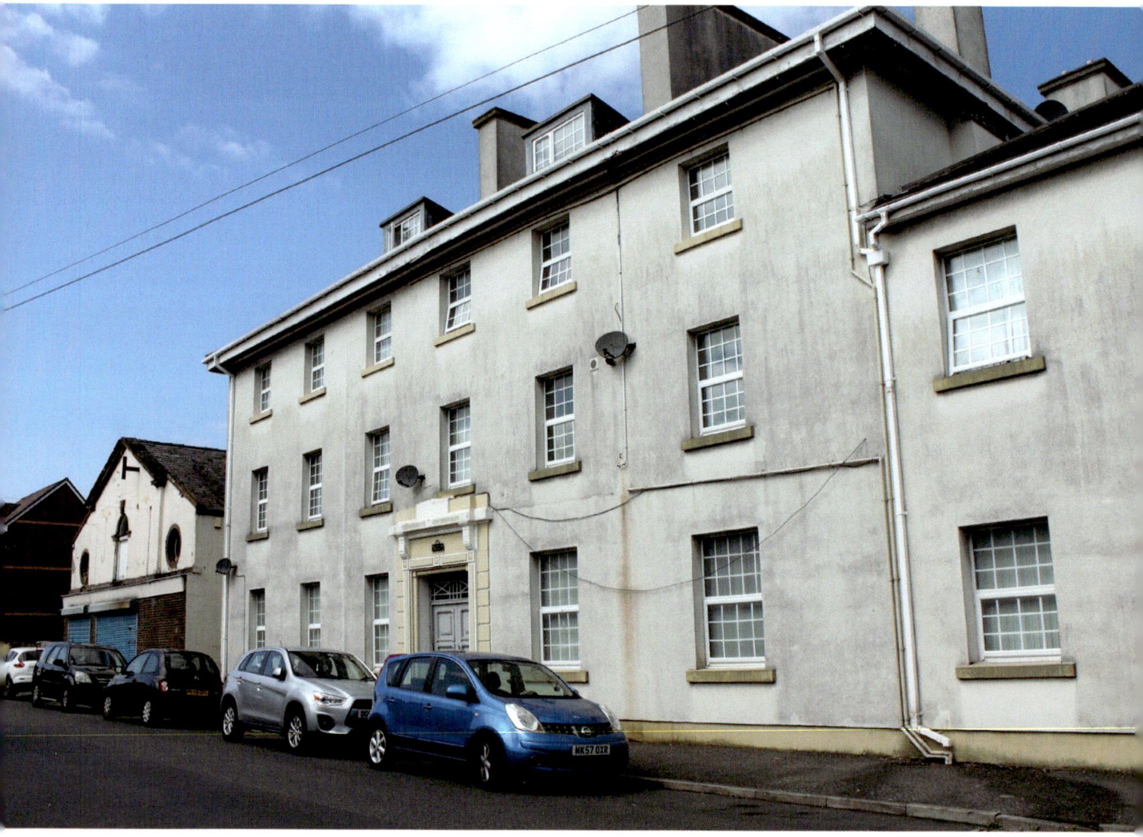

The Albion Hotel after conversion into flats.

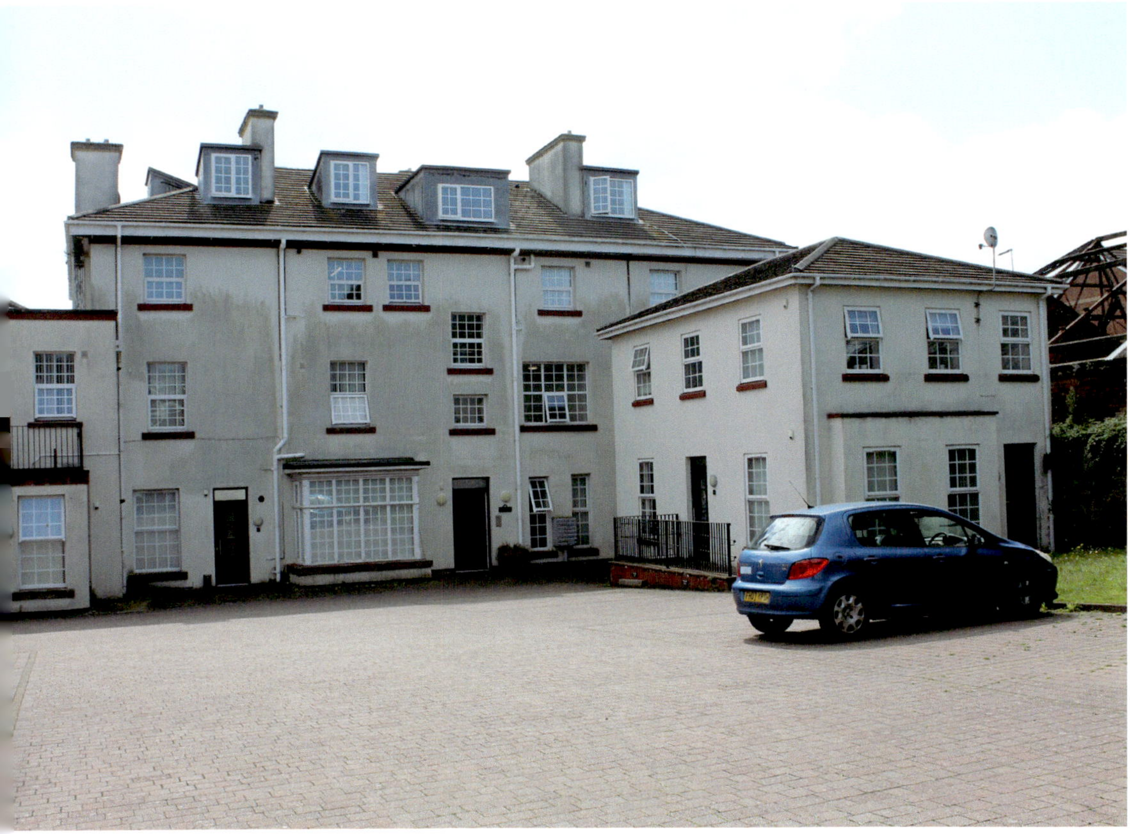

Rear view of The Albion, once a popular beer garden.

1970s when it catered for three distinct groups of drinkers. In the large lounge the older drinkers would while away the evening, leaving the smaller middle room for the 'hairies' and other noisome oiks, whilst the smaller still public bar was where the local bikers congregated, led by a rather intimidating gentleman called 'The Rabbi'. A slightly less menacing customer was General Tom Thumb, who stayed at the Albion when appearing at Reynolds Waxworks in Liverpool.

The pub closed in 2001 and was eventually converted into flats, grandly named Montpelier Mansions after Montpelier Crescent, which runs along the back of the Albion where the large beer garden used to lie, now a car park for the flats.

31. The Swan, Seacombe

Pubs have always attracted nicknames, especially amongst the dockers of Liverpool where every pub had its own amusing sobriquet. The Swan in Seacombe probably has the best on the Wirral side of the Mersey. It was known as The Blazing Stump ever since an unfortunate seafaring patron with a wooden leg tried to poke the fire with his makeshift prosthetic, causing it to catch fire, probably not the brightest thing he had ever done I would venture.

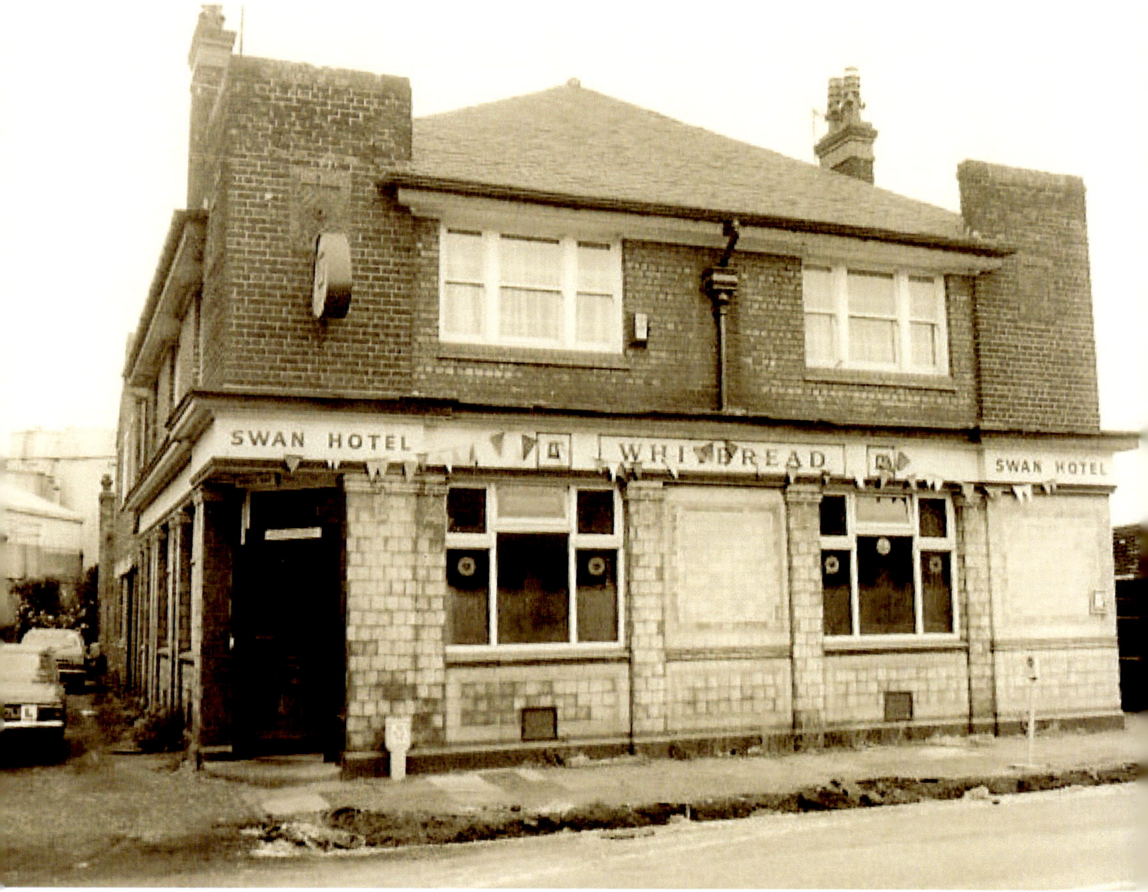

The Swan Hotel as it was in 1978.

Built in 1878 to take advantage of the trade from the nearby Great Float dock system and its hundreds of thirsty dockers, it was billed at the time as having an 'unusual and interesting atmosphere due to the variety of locals and overseas workers who would be visiting at any one time'.

However, it remained a relatively anonymous pub until the 1990s when it was opened up as a nightclub called Bonkers, which was popular enough to attract some famous Liverpool footballers and a regular Saturday night crowd. This popularity was not to last, however, and although just about hanging on, it looks as if it might fall into the Dock Road at any moment.

32. The Grand Trunk, Birkenhead

Built in 1860, The Grand Trunk Hotel was named after the recently completed Grand Trunk Canal, which was established to form a link between the River Mersey and the River Trent, thus opening up the Midlands to additional trade. It was one of dozens of pubs in the so-called grid-iron of streets constructed in the early days of

Birkenhead's expansion and survived longer than most, finally closing its doors in the early 2000s.

Although now converted into flats, two of the three sides of the pub retain the original stone lettering on their facias. The Old Bidston Road side reads 'Grand Trunk Hotel' and if one looks closely the original brewery roundel with 'Birkenhead Ales' and their trademark Liver bird perched on a barrel of beer can just be made out high up on the building. There is another roundel on the Duke Street side and underneath it reads 'Birkenhead Brewery Co. Ltd'. The third side in Brook Street used to bear the legend 'Peerless Ales, Wines & Spirits' until some nameless numbskull came along and hacked it all off.

There is now only one door to the property where there were three, two being blocked off during the conversion into flats. Many pubs had doors on every side and

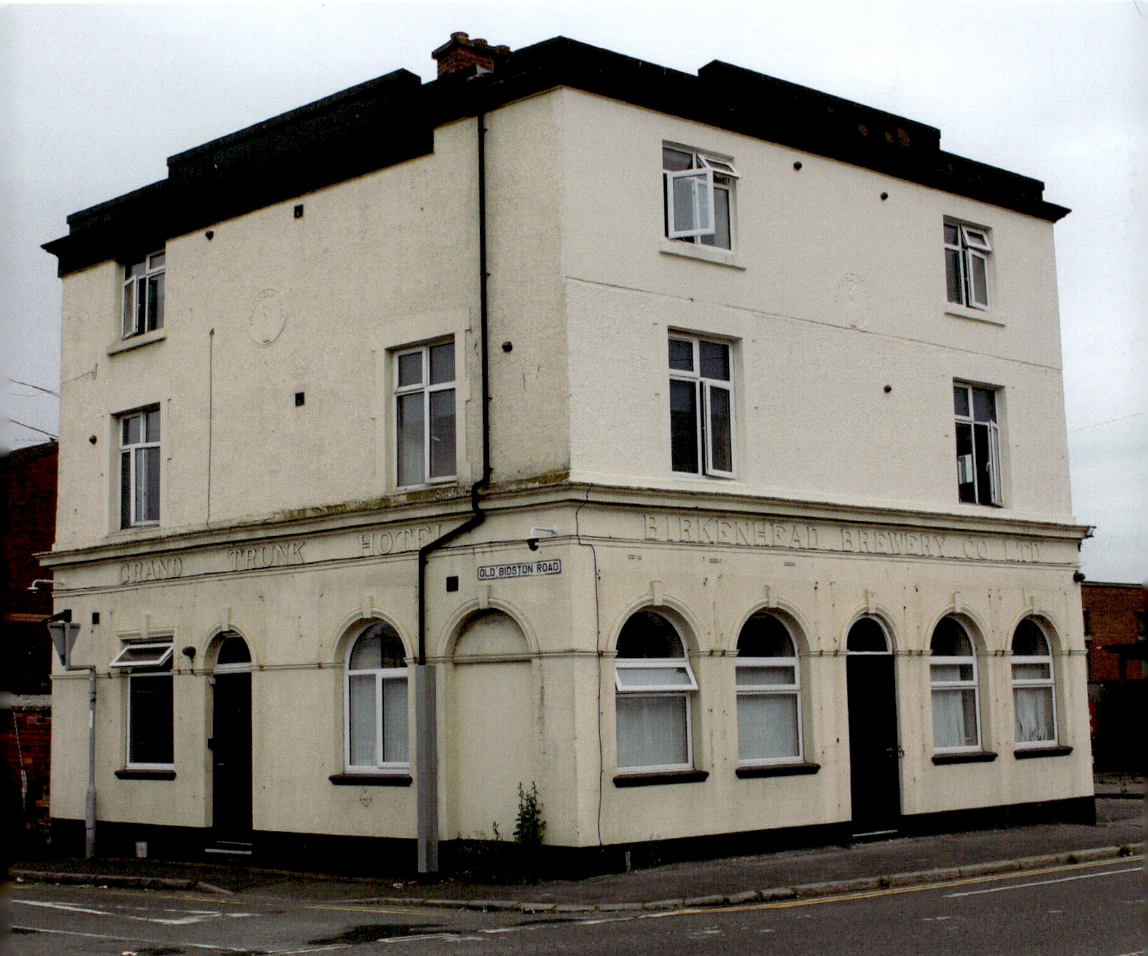

The Grand Trunk Hotel after conversion into flats.

it was thought by some that this was not just a handy way to enter the pub, but a convenient means of escape in the case of a stay-behind that had been rumbled by the local coppers.

33. The Meadows, Birkenhead

The name of this pub strikes a rather ironic note nowadays but when it was constructed in 1870 the area was still mainly green fields and had been since the monks of Birkenhead Priory had tended the area from the 1200s and earlier. Similar in design to The Grand Trunk, it was a little grander, and a little larger, tricked out in fancy designs made from brown, gold and claret coloured faience tiles on the ground floor and 'The Meadows' still visible in stone on the Conway Street and Watson Street sides. The trapdoor down to the cellar, known locally as Scooters House, is also still extant.

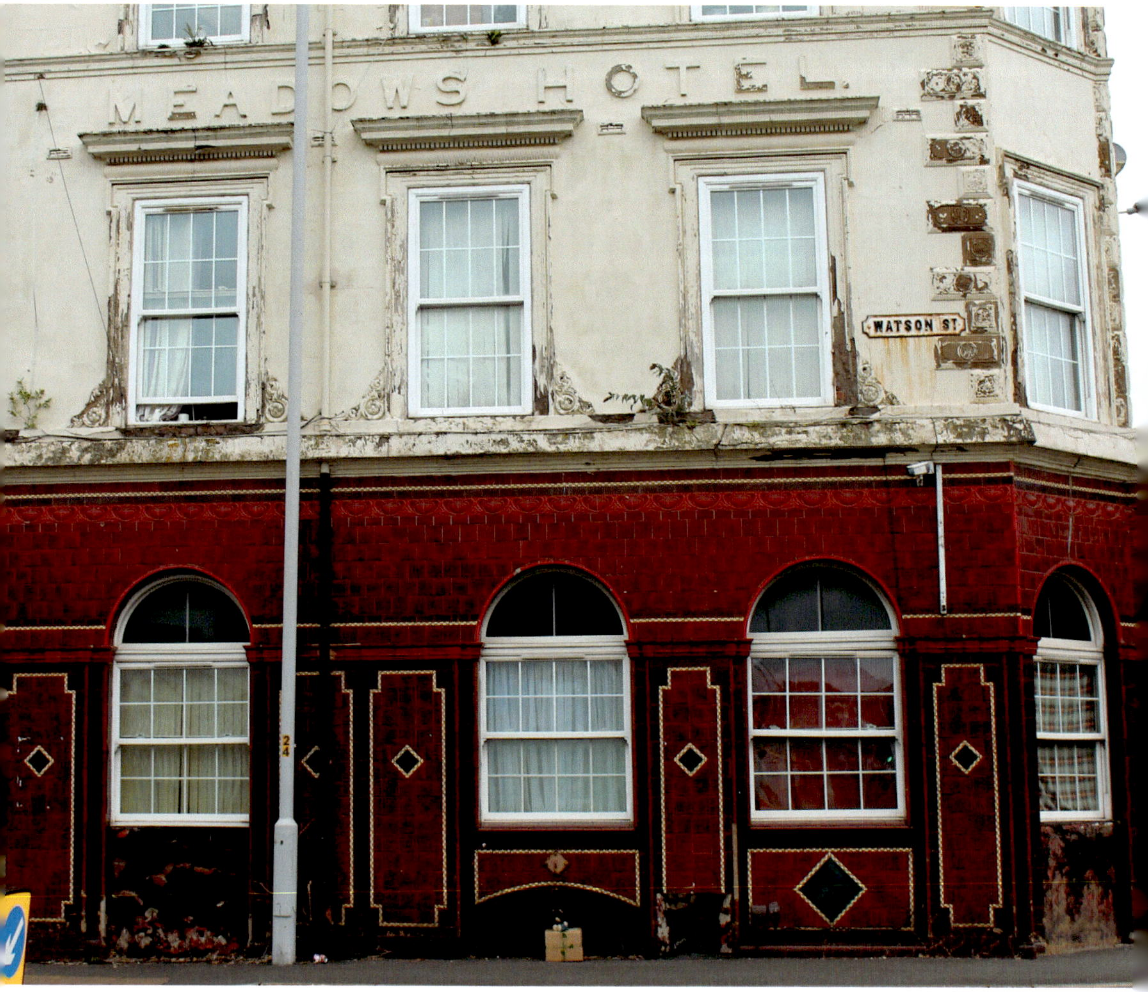

The Meadows in 2024 after conversion.

The building also benefits from the retention of the original window drip moulds and the keystones above the windows on the second floor.

The Meadows is another example of the 'pub on every corner' district that Birkenhead became. The grand designs for the town by the construction of the once-splendid Queens Hotel further down Conway Street and the impressive entrance to Birkenhead Park opposite bear witness to what was envisaged, but unfortunately the town ran out of money and less imposing buildings were constructed in their stead.

34. The Pier Hotel, Birkenhead

In its heyday the Pier Hotel must have appeared to be the archetypal pub, the sort Andy Capp and Chalkie might have frequented. It is, however, so much more than that, due to the retained signage around each side of the building. The Hamilton

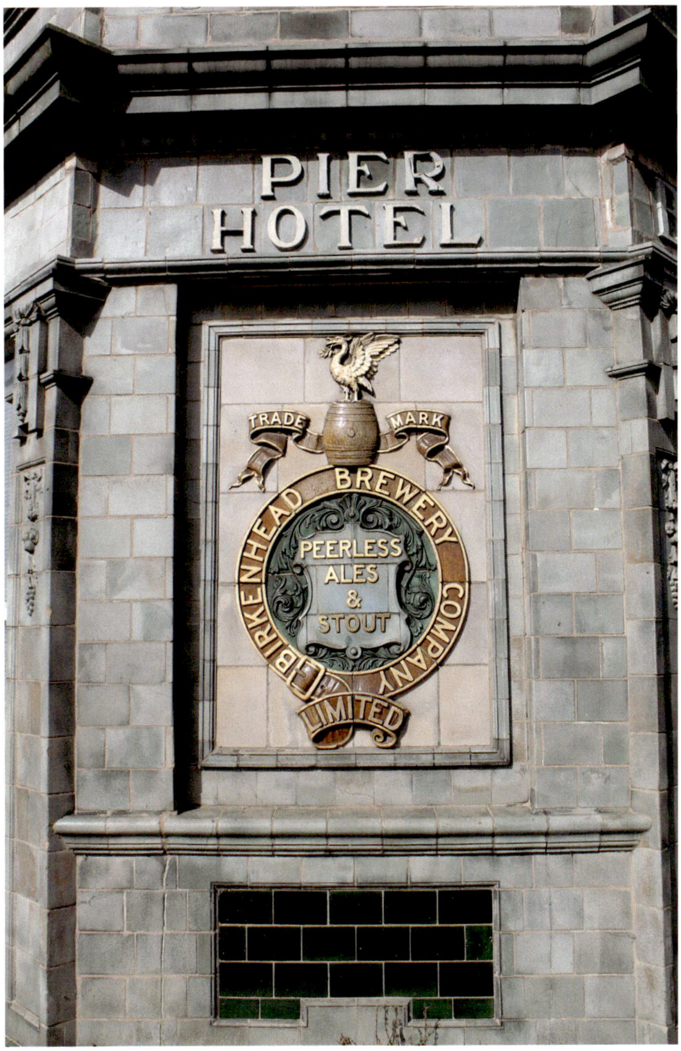

The Birkenhead Brewery crest on the side of the Pier Hotel.

Street side declares 'Birkenhead Ales and Stout' while the Canning Street façade has 'Birkenhead Brewery Co. Ltd.' The *pièce de résistance* lies between the angle of the two: a Birkenhead Brewery sign emblazoned on the side in all its glory. Under the 'Pier Hotel' lettering stands the trademark Liver bird on a beer barrel. Below this lies an escutcheon with 'Peerless Ales and Stout' in gold lettering, surrounded by a claret label with 'Birkenhead Brewery Company Limited' again in gold. Other similar signs survive in the town but this is the finest example by far.

The three-bay stucco villa still standing next door in Canning Street was once part of the pub and boasted 3-foot-high facia boards advertising the hotel, large enough for passengers alighting from the nearby Woodside Ferry to see.

It is therefore a great shame that, whilst retaining the façade of the pub was an enlightened thing to do, the later buildings that encase the pub do not do its architecture justice as they appear to be thrown together with little thought from pieces left over from a child's Lego box.

35. The Chetwynd Arms, Oxton

There are no clues to guide any budding pub sleuths to the fact that the Chetwynd Arms ever existed. The building, however, is still there as part of Bidston Road, the main road through from Oxton to Bidston Hill. Most people will not give it a second glance as it is set back in a lengthy garden tucked away from the busy road. At one time, for a few years in the 1890s, this was the hub of the community.

The former Chetwynd Arms in Bidston Road.

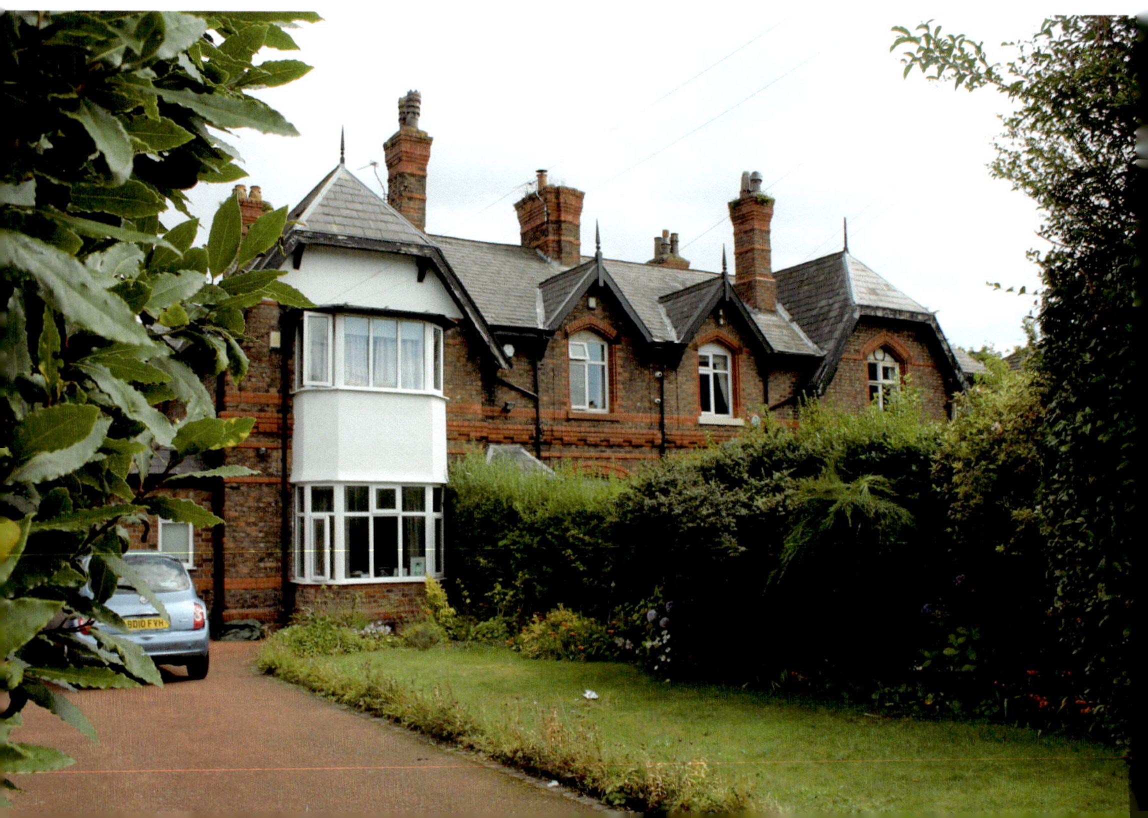

Opening as a licensed premises in 1877, its original name gives a clue as to the reason for its existence. Known as the Quarrymans Arms, it was patronised by a large workforce labouring away in the many quarries once located hereabouts. The nearest and largest was the Lingdale Quarry, located to the east of where Brancote Road now stands. Evidence of the quarry can still be seen in some of the back gardens of the large houses in the road. Further trade came from the workers at the smaller quarries located between Heather Brow and Lingdale Road, and to the north of Lingdale Road North where Valerian Road now stands.

Henry Mutch owned Lingdale quarry and also built Nos 1–4 Mutches Cottages, aka The Quarrymans Arms – he was quite the entrepreneur. As a nod to the major landowner, the Earl of Shrewsbury – full name Charles Henry John Benedict Crofton Chetwynd Chetwynd-Talbot no less – the pub changed its name to the Chetwynd Arms but this did not prevent its closure in 1891.

36. The Ring O' Bells, Bidston

This is another former pub that gives no clues as to its origins as a licensed premises. It was run by a succession of Radleys and Pembertons until one Simon Croft took over the reins and established a reputation for his first-rate ham and eggs, keeping pigs at the back of the pub for this purpose. Unfortunately, his business success was also his downfall as he succumbed to the temptation of the demon drink and became an alcoholic.

Church Farm in Bidston, formerly The Ring O' Bells pub.

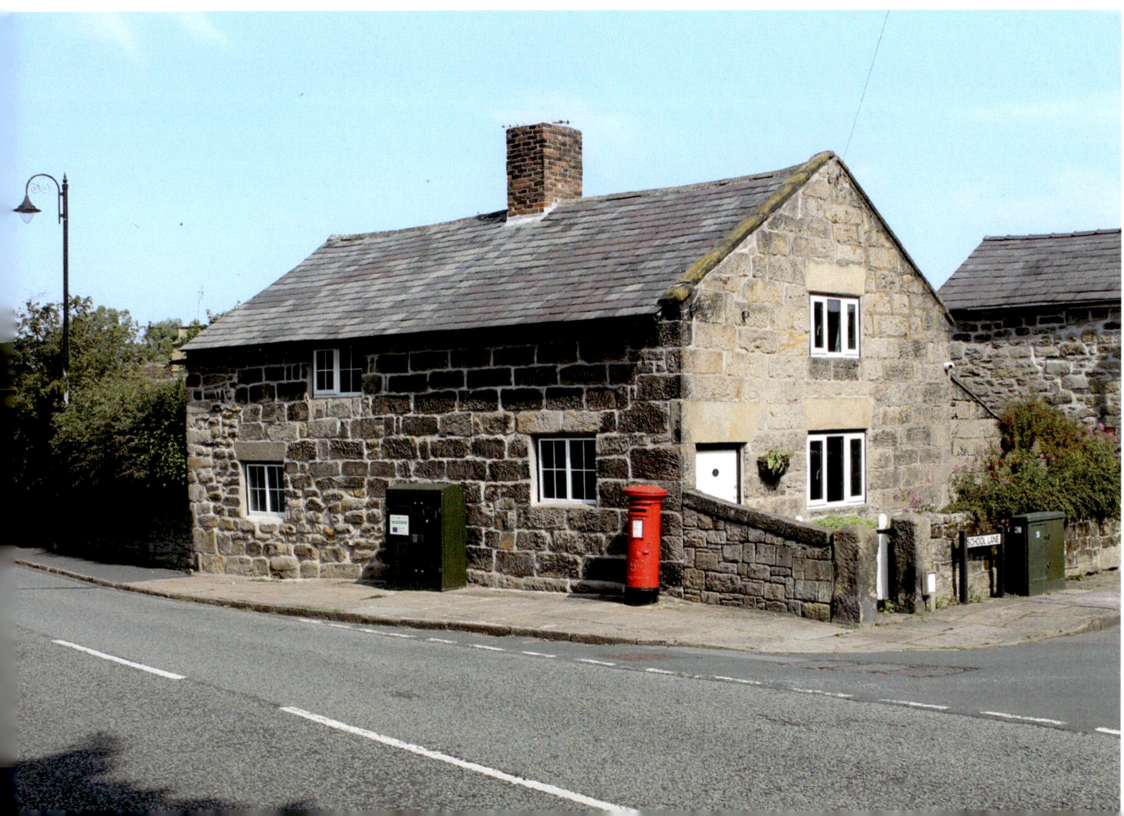

The pub never gave any tick to its patrons. The modern notice 'please do not ask for credit as a punch in the face often offends' was spelled out more poetically on a large sign above the bar, which read:

Walk in my friend and taste my beer and liquor.
If your pockets be well stored you'll find it comes quicker.
But for want of that which causes both grief and sorrow,
You must pay today, I will trust tomorrow!

Licensed in 1750, it was the only pub in the village and as a consequence it attracted what was described as a 'lively and mixed crowd, including prize fighters Tom Sayers, Jem Mace and The Tipton Slasher'. You get the picture.

This was all too much for the god-fearing folk of Bidston, especially when a herd of drunks were found sleeping off the previous night's excesses in the nearby graveyard. The pub closed in 1868 and became Stone Farm, which it remains to this day.

37. The Dog and Gun, Bebington

This was once a Birkenhead Brewery pub but only held a licence to sell beer but not spirits or wine. Drinkers had to look elsewhere for their favourite tipple. Closed way back in 1910, it became the village post office and latterly a betting shop. After being

The old Dog and Gun pub in Bebington.

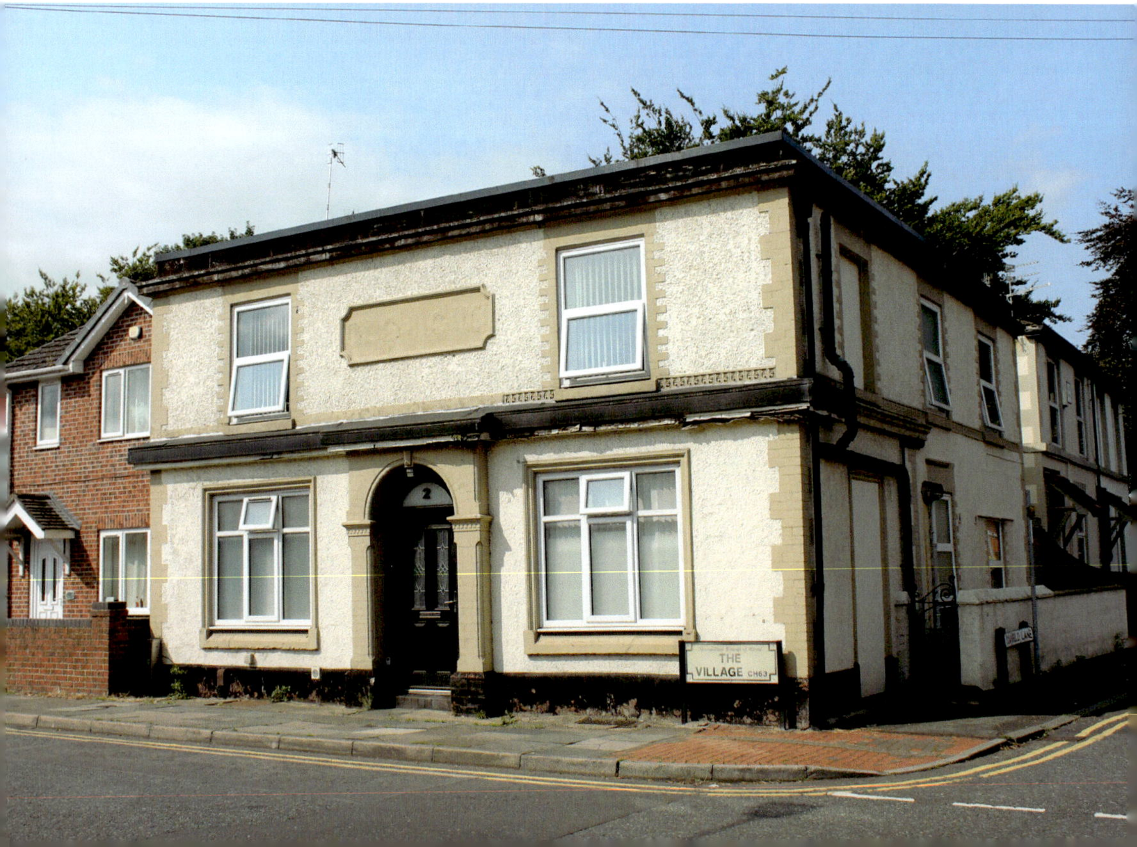

left empty and deteriorating, as so often happens, it was finally renovated and turned into flats during which time the overall appearance was spruced up and the horrible shutters that someone had seen fit to deface the building with were replaced by a window, now in keeping with the rest of the property. The Dog and Gun lettering can still be made out on the panel above the front door on The Village side.

There is the standard blocked door to the Townfeld Lane side where two cottages built contemporaneously with the pub remain. The nearest one to the pub sports a small date stone giving the year of construction as 1851, along with the owner's initials.

38. The Gladstone Arms, Bebington

Constructed in 1875, The Gladstone Arms was named as a nod to Lord Lever, who constructed Port Sunlight nearby, was a devout Liberal all his life and was good friends with the Liberal Party leader William Ewart Gladstone, whose name is also remembered at the Gladstone Theatre in the village. There is excellent stone signage on the south wall of the premises declaring its original function and indeed still retains most of its original external features.

There is a large segmental arched window to Bromborough Road and attractive quoins at each corner, painted white to contrast well with the darker render of

The Gladstone Arms in 2024.

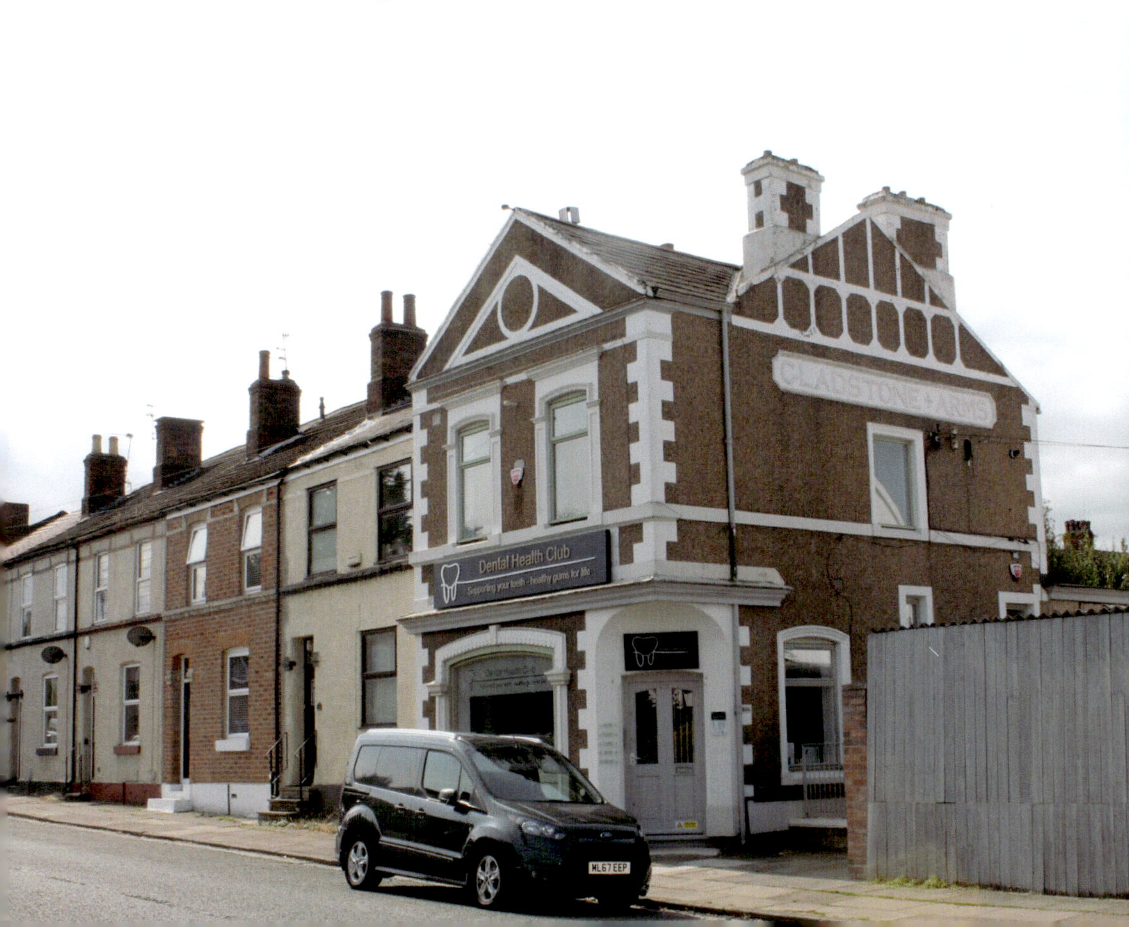

the building. Even the chimneys above received this treatment. Both gables retain fancy features, although they were a slightly later addition to the décor, and the two upstairs windows boast fluted surrounds, again in brilliant white. The former occupiers of the Gladstone Arms were a firm of builders who clearly used the property to advertise their business. The current owners have continued to look after the historic property.

The pub closed in 1955 when the Brown Cow (confusingly known as Gladstones) opened its doors, with the licence from the Gladstone being transferred over to the Cow. This in turn closed and has since been demolished, with flats now occupying the site.

39. The Royal Oak, Bebington

Not as easy to spot as a former pub than the previous two mentioned above, although the building does still sport an original hanging sign, albeit bearing the name of the current business occupying the property. In 1880 the Birkenhead Brewery bought four cottages on Village Road and opened the central two as The Royal Oak, one of which

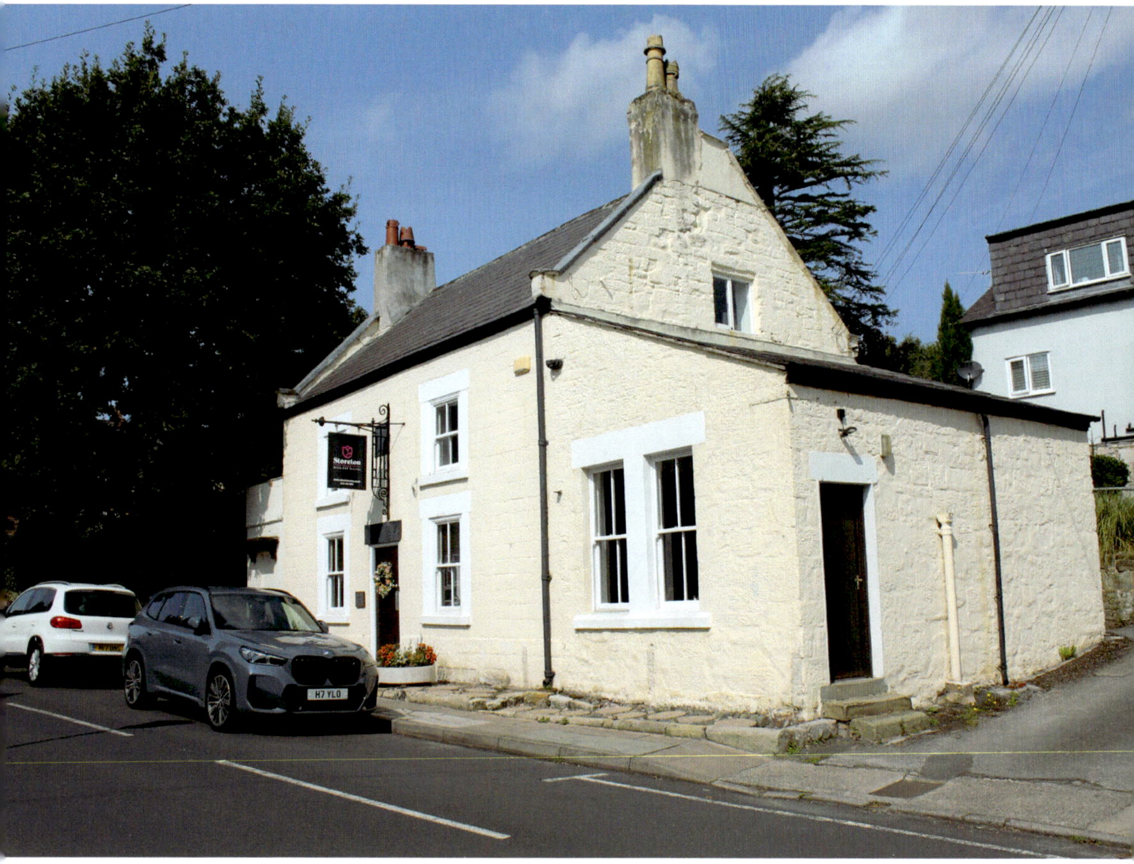

The Royal Oak in Village Road as it is today.

bore a date stone of 1739, which still survives to the left of the hanging sign. The whole property remains incredibly unchanged from a photograph taken of the pub in the 1880s, even down to the small wooden fence outside. The only slight alterations have been to the sloping roof to the right, which possibly housed a hay loft but has had a pair of sashes inserted, happily in keeping with the original windows.

Closed in 1960, the valuable licence was transferred to the recently completed and much larger Acorn down the road in Teehey Lane. It was said at the time that when the old pub shut and the new one opened, the popular saying had been turned on its head, namely 'From tiny Oaks, mighty Acorns grow'.

40. The Red Lion, Willaston

There is only one pub remaining in Willaston. The Nags Head nestles on the sharp bend in Neston Road as it snakes through the village. Look across the Green to the west, however, and a large half-timbered building looms into view. Originally built as two separate houses in 1631, the buildings were knocked into one and became The Red Lion pub in 1822. The ubiquitous Birkenhead Brewery took over the running of

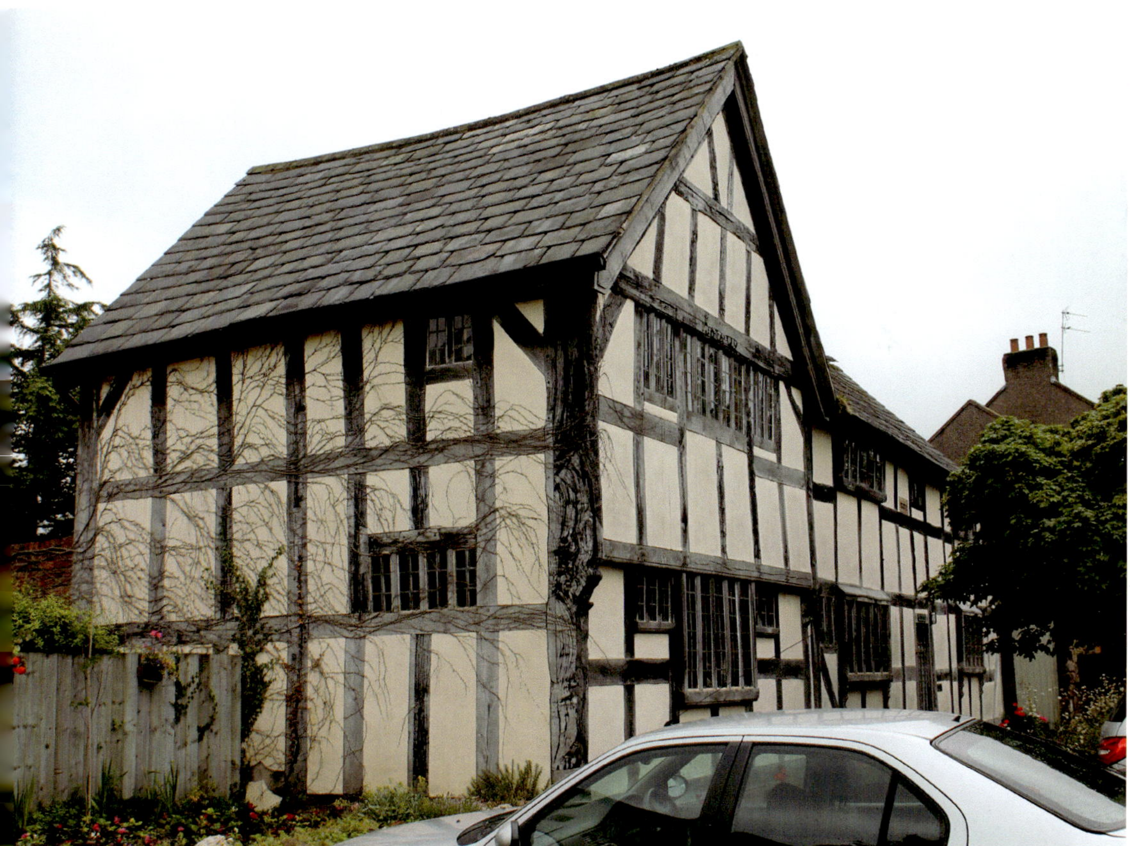

The buildings that once housed The Red Lion in Willaston.

this country pub in 1902 and it remained a popular watering hole for the locals for decades to come. Unfortunately, a property of this size requires passing trade, which The Red Lion was ill-positioned to do and it closed its doors in 1963.

The brewery applied to have the pub demolished and planning permission was sought to put up one of those execrable 1960s 'taverns' that would surely have blighted the village for evermore. The villagers therefore had a lucky escape when permission was refused and the Green returned to its sleepy reverie once more. The Red Lion was converted back to residential use.

41. The Coach and Horses, Neston

Neston was once the most important town in Wirral before the development of Birkenhead in the 1820s, with no fewer than eleven pubs available to the thirsty locals. It was also the main route through from Chester and North Wales to Liverpool and the north-west for the mail coaches, which required regular stops to change over horses and feed and water passengers. This is the reason that so many pubs were called The

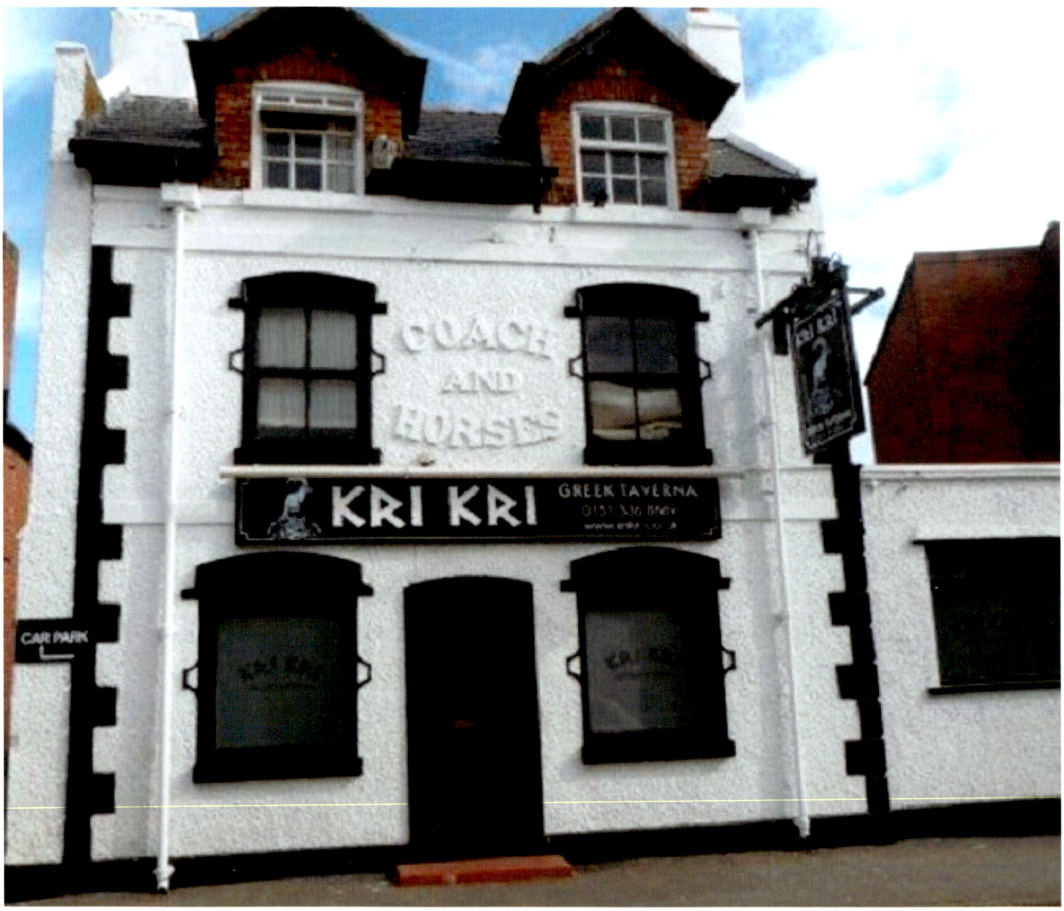

The old Coach and Horses pub in Neston, now a Greek restaurant.

Coach and Horses – no fewer than 111 so named still exist in Britain. The Neston example provided such a service from 1822 onwards, gleaning trade for many years from travellers, locals and from the local market, which came to town on a weekly basis. The pub was never large, unlike many other coaching inns, but managed to expand into the small cottage next door.

The building looks similar to The Gladstone Arms in Bebington with its segmental front windows and quoins. The original lettering is still clearly visible above the sign for a Greek restaurant called Kri Kri (a mountain goat apparently), which it became in 2013 after the pub was closed down permanently in 2008.

Lost Pubs

There are so many pubs in Wirral that have disappeared without a scrap of evidence to tell of their existence, other than in the memories of an ever-dwindling band of drinkers that laughed, joked, chatted or fell over in these special places. When a pub is pulled down, it is not just an inconvenient building that is being destroyed. It is the collective experiences of thousands of ordinary people who came together to socialise, with friends, strangers and future partners; for fun, watching the Coronation, the football, or the rugby; for collective celebration, weddings, birthdays, or Dave's new car; or for collective grief, funerals, the death of Churchill, or the break-up of Take That. Pubs, especially on Merseyside, are seldom lonely places; there is always someone to chat to at the bar, whether it's the sympathetic ear of the bar staff or just a fellow customer hoping for a natter.

So here are a few of these special places. They represent hundreds that are gone but not forgotten, reminders to us all that we must appreciate this uniquely British institution, and to utilise and treasure what is left. Cheers.

42. The Hotel Victoria, New Brighton

New Brighton, rather like Port Sunlight fifty years later, began life as the vision of a wealthy and driven man, in this case James Atherton, who's dream was to turn the windblown sands of the North Wirral coast into a clean, healthy, attractive place to live for the many well-to-do merchants that worked across the water in Liverpool, amongst the grime and smells of a full-on version of the Industrial Revolution. Each inhabitant was to enjoy their own unique view of the bay on the steeply rising land, with the higher ground, and some of the best views, reserved for the lucky few residing in The Hotel Victoria.

Built in 1837, this distinctive yellow brick building was a local landmark until its sad demise in 2006, and boasted the usual Victorian array of features to attract the well-heeled client. Hot and cold water (but not yet any en-suite facilities), a large drinking area and a luxurious ballroom. It attracted the famous, including Emmeline Pankhurst and Charles Blondin, and the infamous, notably the murderer Dr Hawley

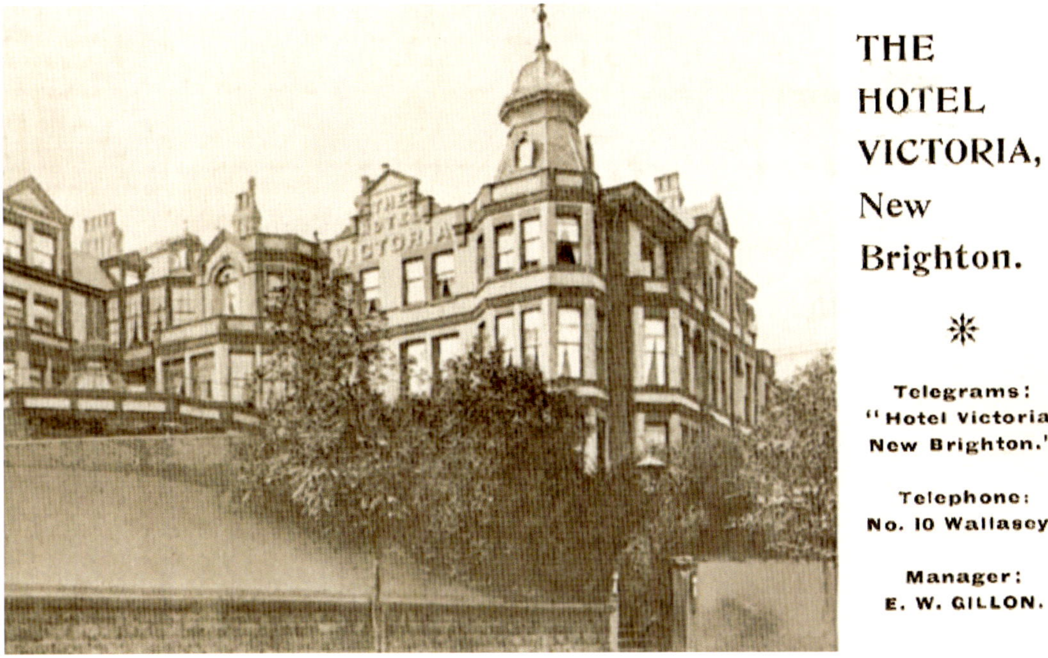

The Hotel Victoria advertised on an old postcard.

Harvey Crippen, who gave a lecture on electrical massage, which in his hands was probably as dangerous as it sounds. Its comprehensive destruction was an awful loss to the area but it proved impossible to repurpose such a large building and flats were eventually built on what remains a prime site.

43. The Dale, Seacombe

Some pubs seem to have been with us forever. The Dale was not one of these – blink and you missed it. Opened in the 1970s, it was gone before the 1990s were out. For those of a certain age, however, it was THE place to be as it established a reputation for putting on local bands, especially during the week when things were usually pretty quiet on the pub front. There was a large bar area to the left but all the hairies made their way to the right and into the large circular area where the bands played. I remember with great fondness being hit over the head with a flying microphone launched into the sweaty throng by the perpetually angry lead singer of Attempted Moustache, who were lively precursors of the thrash metal scene. Bernard Manning is also said to have performed a few charity gigs here at the time.

Many people will remember the large rocking horse hanging from the ceiling. This wasn't stuck there just for a laugh; the original idea was to call the pub The Carousel and our equine friend would have been part of the theme. No reason has been found as to why this did not happen, but they settled on The Dale to perpetuate the memory of a pub of the same name that stood nearby in Oakdale Road. The site is now a Tesco Express.

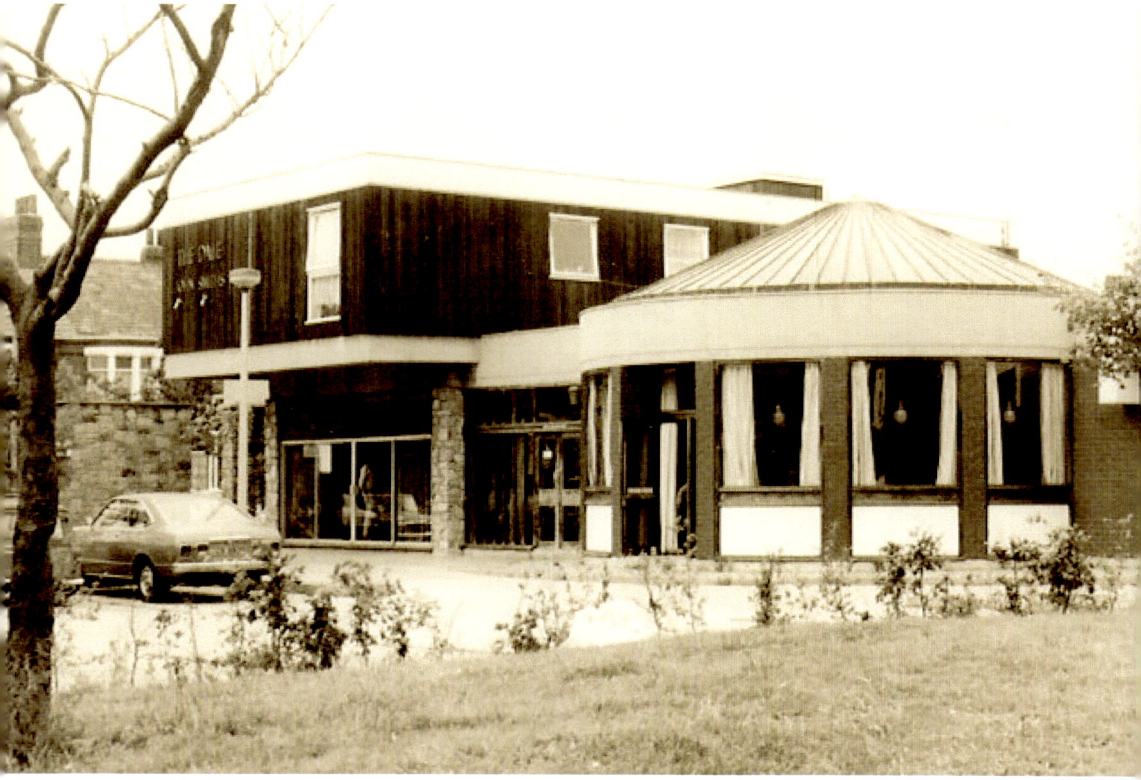

The Dale in Seacombe in 1978.

44. The Jolly Sailor, Poulton

Poulton seems to have had more than its fair share of pub, but it now has one. The reason for the high number of licenced premises was the trade from the nearby Great Float dock system and the constant stream of thirsty sailors hanging about waiting for their ship to sail. There was such a large contingent of seafarers from the subcontinent that the whole area became known as the Indian Village.

Opened in 1882, The Jolly Sailor provided the background for a salutary tale related to me many years ago. It involved a group of sailors who had been drinking in the pub since opening time. Pubs in those days were legally obliged to close during the afternoon, so one of the merry tars suggested going back to his nearby digs where they continued to drink from a wooden barrel one of them had 'liberated' from one of the ships. The contents tasted a little odd but it was clearly alcoholic so no one seemed to mind, but as the contents were being consumed the barrel seemed to remain a little heavier than it should. To get to the last dregs, a hammer and chisel were called for and with one or two lusty blows the keg split open and out plopped a pickled monkey, destined for a laboratory but now laid out on the horrified sailors' kitchen floor in a pool of cheap brandy. This no doubt sobered them all up rather quickly.

The pub closed in 1924 and was demolished in 1961.

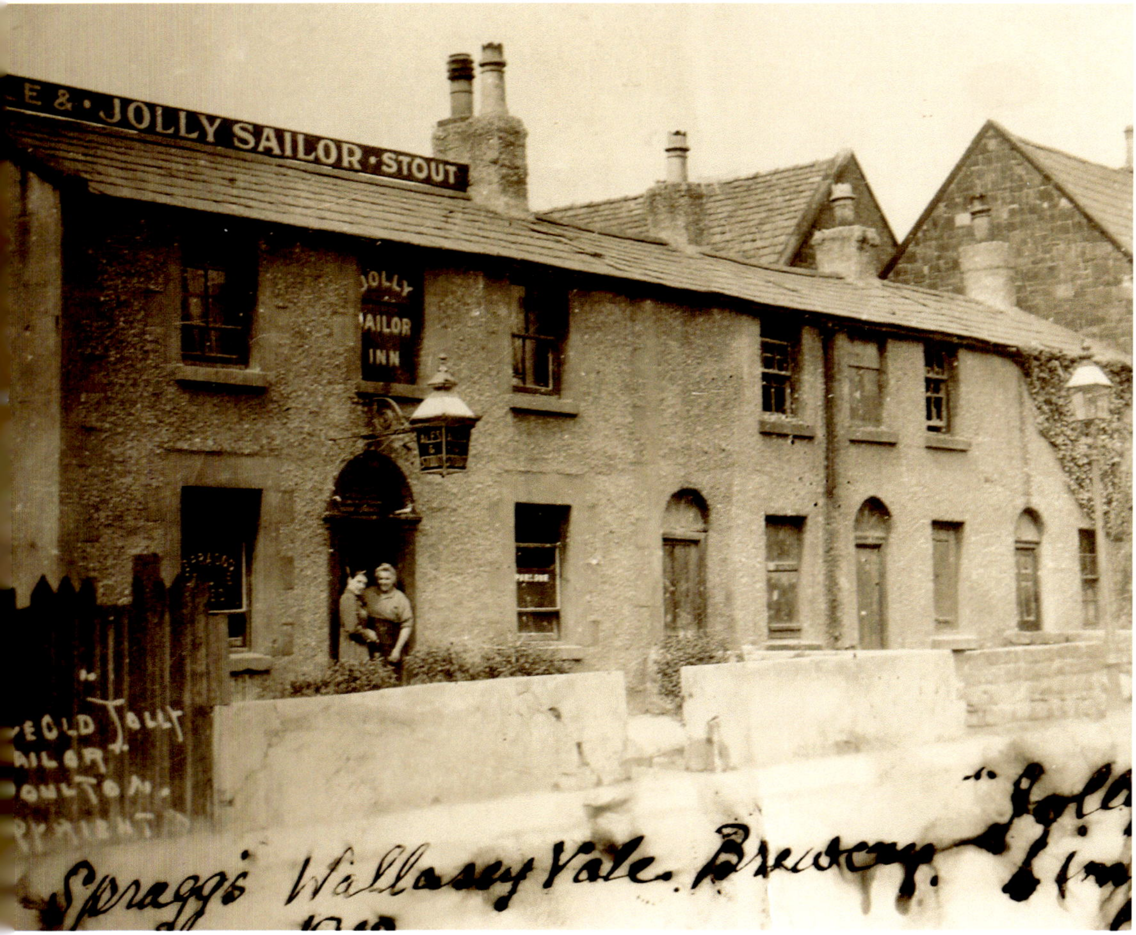

The Jolly Sailor on an old postcard from 1911.

45. The Grange, Birkenhead

A rather strange thing has crept into pub etiquette over the past few years and I may have found the root cause. Since time immemorial patrons have stood at the bar waiting to be served; everyone knew what to do, everyone waited patiently and woe betide anyone who jumped in before their turn. Nowadays it is common practice to form a queue at right angles to the bar! When did this suddenly become a thing? Then in my addled brain I came up with a theory. Maybe it stems from The Grange Hotel being pulled down in 1982 and replaced with a McDonalds? Maybe the queueing etiquette of McDonalds has transferred itself into the queueing behaviour of pubs? Whatever next?

'A half of mild please landlord'.
'Do you want to go large?'
'Yes ok, I'll have a pint'.

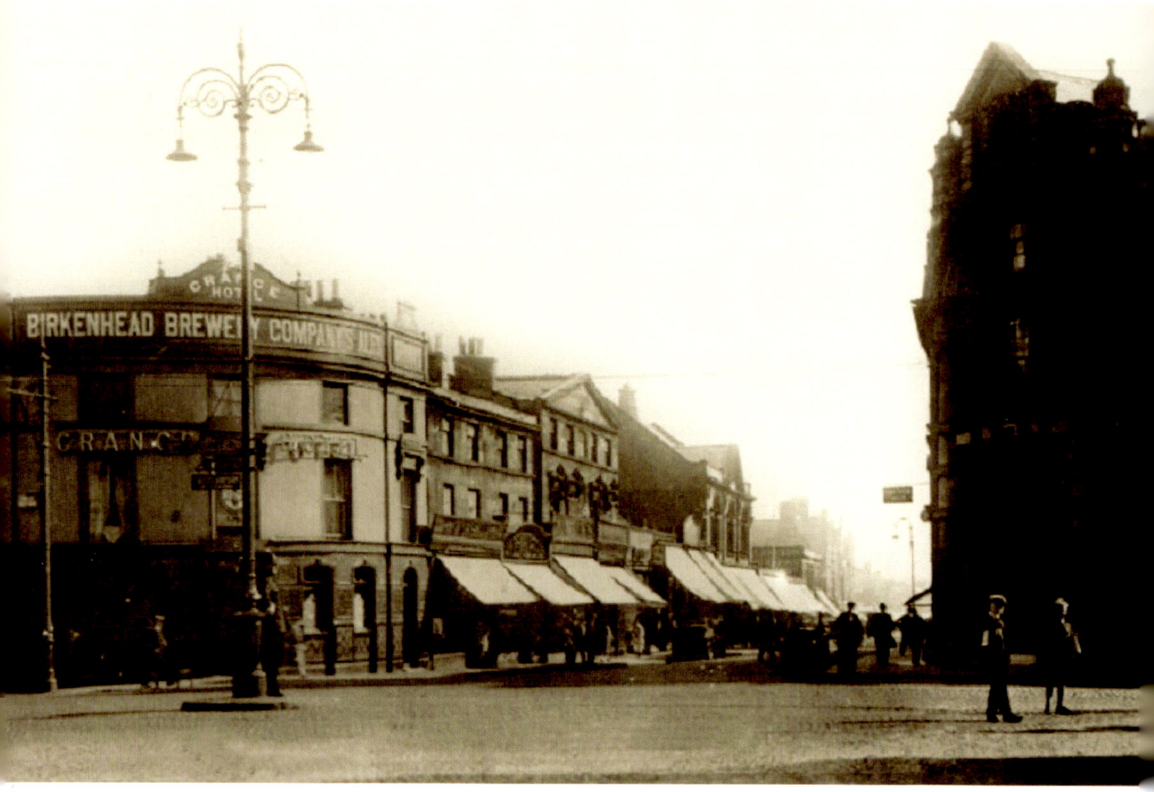

The Grange at Charing Cross around 1910.

Opening in 1850, The Grange Hotel was a perfect example of how a pub should be built to turn a long corner. It was designed with elegant charm, faintly Italianate with a marvellous faience band at the bottom incorporating a beautifully moulded horse trough at the side – even our thirsty equine friends were not forgotten. The pub was in such a prominent position on Charing Cross that they saw fit to name it twice, once on a large facia board and again halfway up in large gold lettering. It was a grand building for a grand site. The pub was named after Grange Road, which in turn was named after the route the monks of Birkenhead Priory took to get to their grange or farm, located near where Euston Grove now stands.

46. The Happy Valley, Birkenhead

One of the most popular Birkenhead pubs in the 1970s, The Happy Valley, built in 1864, was named from its position at the foot of a once picturesque valley, described at the time as 'a very pleasant vale with wild primroses covering the banks and a stream known as the Rubicon running down the centre to Tranmere Pool'. Hilda Gamlin in her book of 1892 noted a vast change: 'the locality, which is sadly deteriorated, is now covered with the lowest class of tenement leaving no trace of the sylvan glade'. These houses in turn were swept away in the 1980s

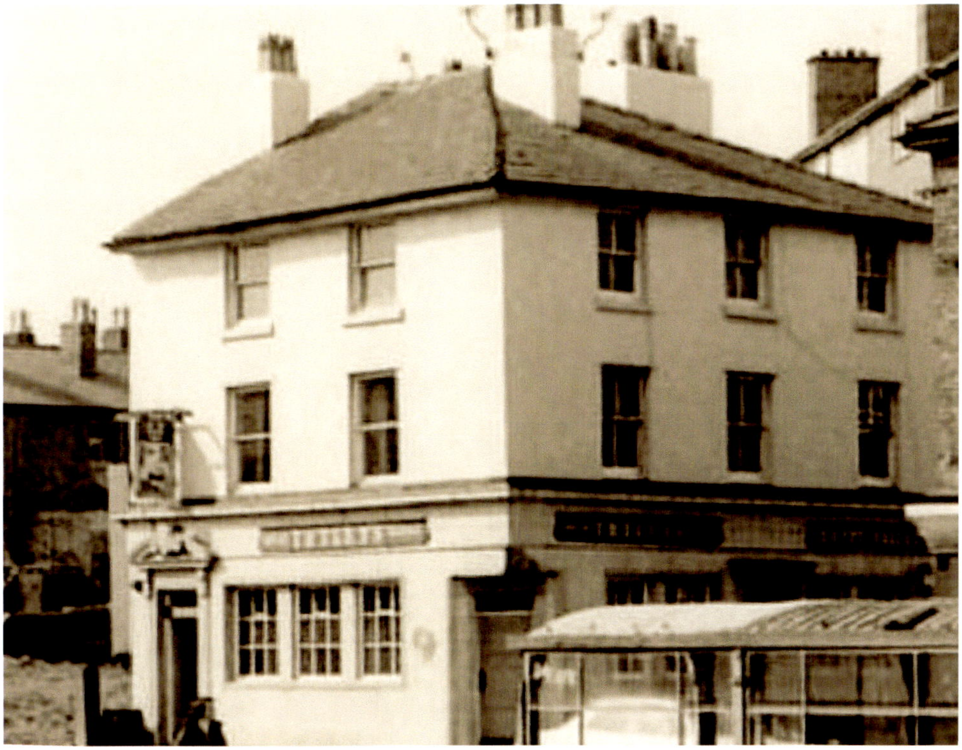

The Happy Valley pub around 1965.

due to road widening, taking The Happy Valley with them when a compulsory purchase order was made for all the property facing Borough Road up to where the Greek restaurant has managed to survive. The site of the pub is now a bus stop opposite the library. There were once nine pubs on Borough Road, but now there is one.

47. The Great Eastern, New Ferry

Named in celebration of Isambard Kingdom Brunel's famous but ill-fated ship, The Great Eastern pub lay to the east of the New Ferry foreshore where ships were laid out for repair or to be dismantled at the end of their useful lives. This was to be the fate of Brunel's great ship when at the end of an eventful career in 1889 it was brought to New Ferry to be taken apart. The owners of the pub did not want to miss the opportunity to own parts of the ship and were successful at auction in obtaining major pieces to adorn the pub lounge. Wood panelling, the ship's wheel and even the ship's bar were brought up from the shore along with a number of stained-glass windows.

None of this memorabilia remained, however, when the pub faced closure, and although a group of locals tried hard to keep the pub going, English Heritage sadly concluded that it was not worth saving as all relics had been taken from the pub,

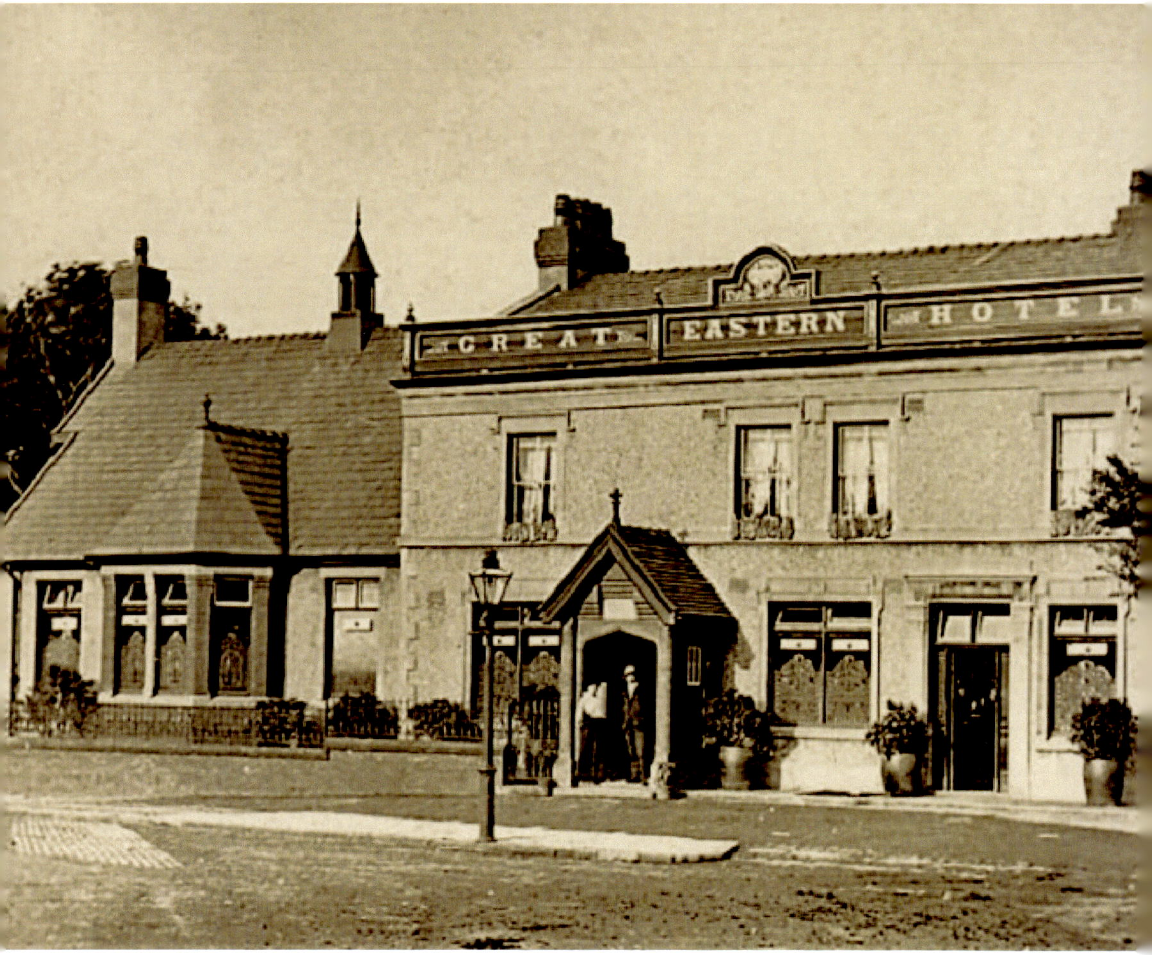

An old postcard view of The Great Eastern.

which in any event had been altered radically since it was built. It closed in 2007 and was demolished in 2010.

There are only a few examples of public houses being completely lost beyond the urban areas of north Wirral as most would have been repurposed or returned to residential use. A good example of this lies in the picturesque village of Burton. Once home to half a dozen pubs with such marvellous names as the Fishermans Arms and The Earth Stomper, all these fine hostelries have reverted to private cottages with no clues as to their historic purpose. Burton now joins the small group of Wirral villages without a pub, namely Brimstage, Puddington, Landican and Shotwick.

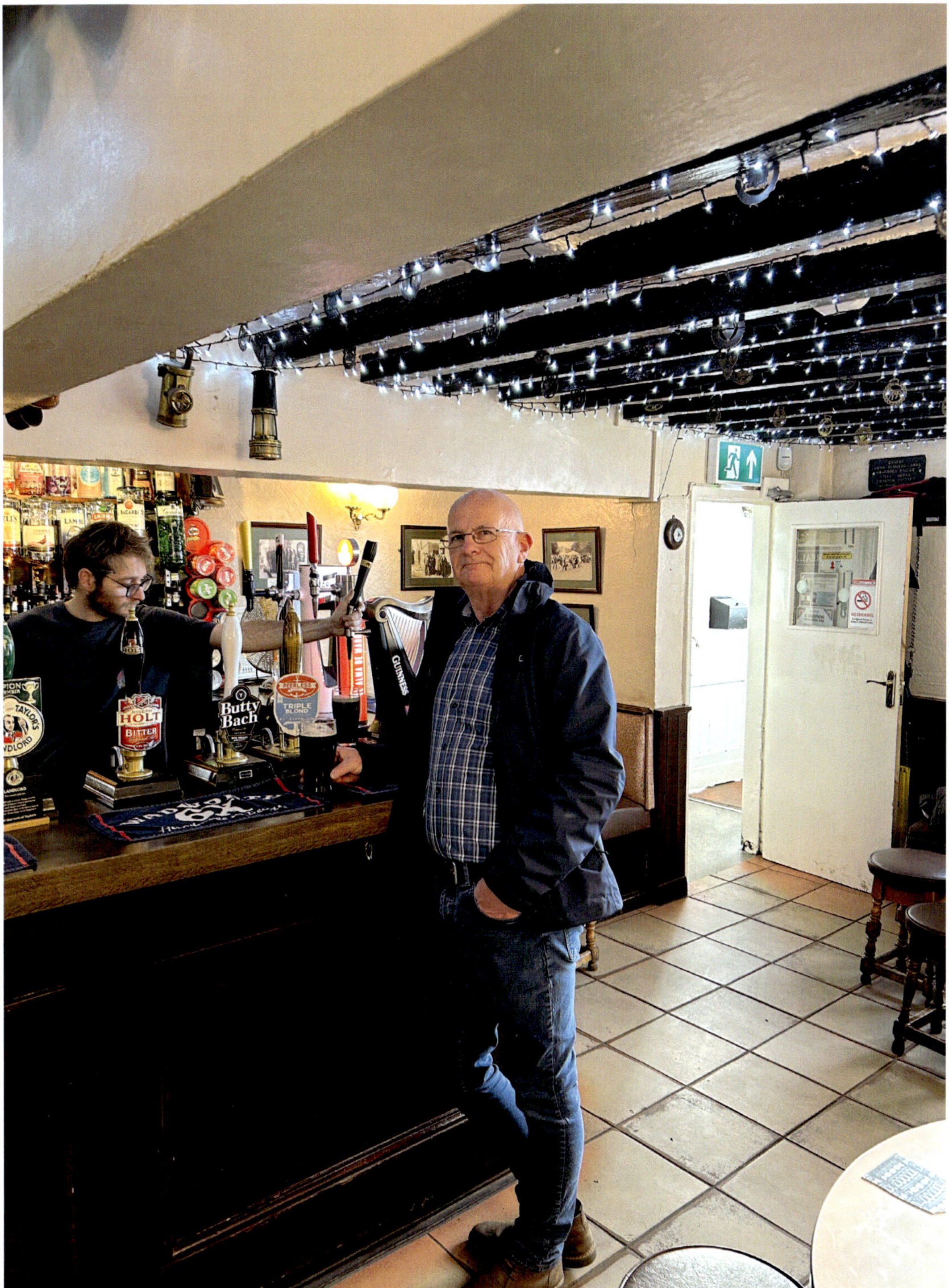

The author with a pint of plum porter at The Harp.

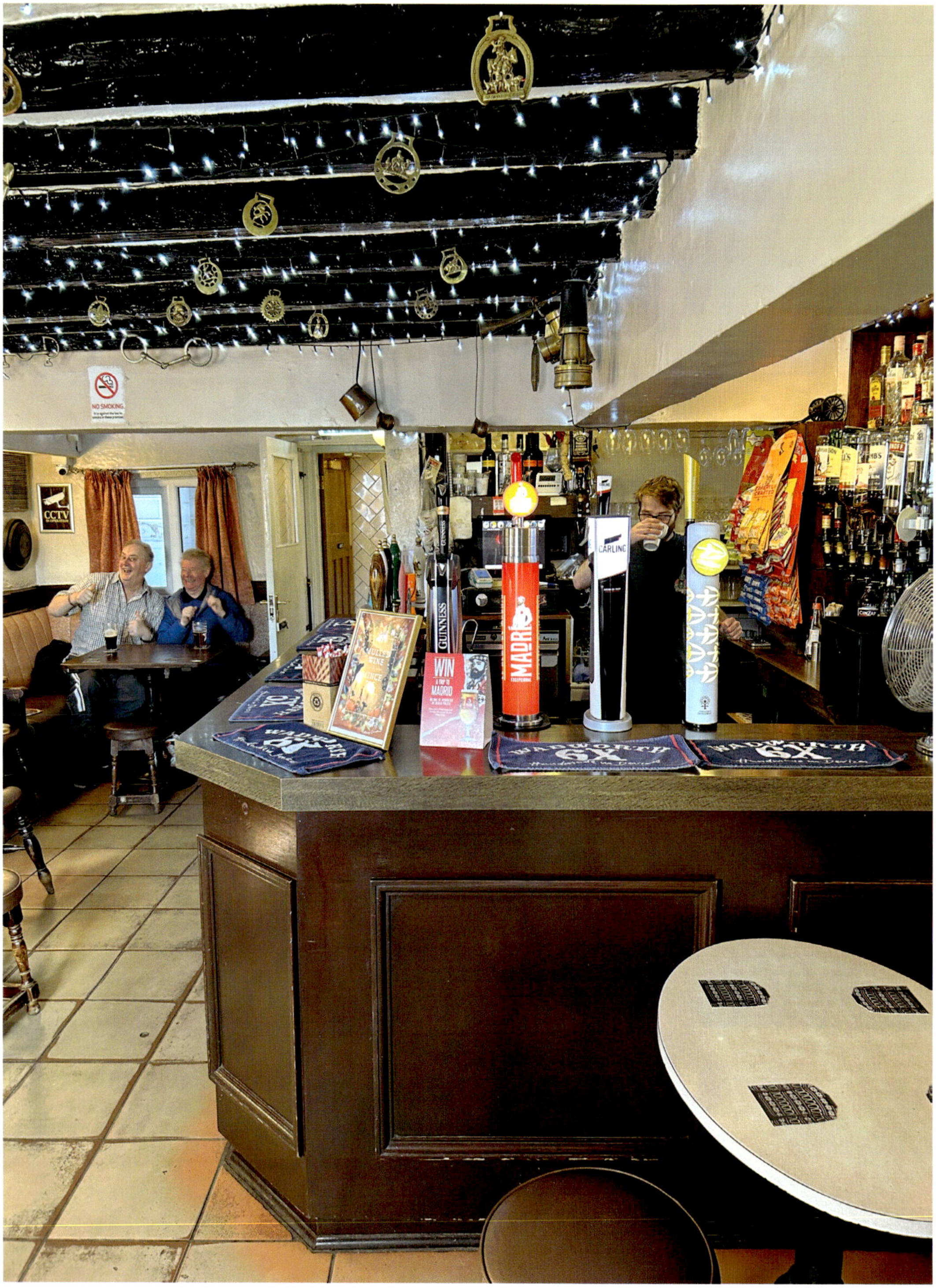

The bar at The Harp and a couple of locals in party mood.